TRUTH *or* TABLOID?®

PETER FENTON

THREE RIVERS PRESS

NEW YORK

This book is dedicated to the unsung heroes of the publishing industry, the humble booksellers, who, now that they have been singled out for praise by me, will shelve *Truth or Tabloid?* face-out in numerous prominent locations and hand-sell it with evangelical fervor at every opportunity, including lunch, afternoon breaks, and while working at Starbucks in order to support their bookselling habit.

Published by Three Rivers Press, New York, New York.

Member of the Crown Publishing Group, a division of Random House, Inc.

www.randomhouse.com

THREE RIVERS PRESS and the Tugboat design are registered trademarks of Random House, Inc.

TRUTH OR TABLOID?® is a registered trademark of Peter Fenton.

Printed in the United States of America

Design by Kay Schuckhart/Blond on Pond

Library of Congress Cataloging-in-Publication Data

Fenton, Peter.

   Truth or tabloid? / Peter Fenton.—1st ed.
  1. Guessing games.   2. Newspapers—Headlines.   3. Tabloid newspapers.   I. Title.
  GV1473.F46   2003
  793.7—dc21   2002006522

ISBN 0-609-80971-7

10 9 8 7 6 5 4 3 2 1

First Edition

CONTENTS

INTRODUCTION

Check out the headlines in any morning newspaper and you'll undoubtedly find one that gives you pause. You wonder, Is this a joke? A hilarious put-on created by an editorial prankster? But reading the story, you learn the outrageous headline is, unfortunately for the human race, all-too-true.

TRUTH _or_ TABLOID?® is your chance to test your talent for separating the bizarre from the bogus, the unreal from the all-too-real.

This is your opportunity to match wits with a half-wit—legendary supermarket tabloid reporter Nigel Puddingporne. Are Nigel's wild headlines true? Or are they the product of his fevered, Guinness-enhanced imagination? You decide.

Nigel burned the midnight oil, and what remained of his brain cells, to create a massive one hundred games and a whopping five hundred headlines to challenge your media-saturated mind. They are cleverly broken into ten categories corresponding to the sections in a typical daily newspaper—from gossip to lifestyles to business and sports—with trivia-filled answers from impeccable sources and Nigel's trenchant commentary.

Each game contains five headlines. Score yourself on the number of headlines you identify correctly as either "Truth" or "Tabloid" by consulting the following table:

0 out of 5 correct: It's cold and wet in your cave.

1 out of 5 correct: Smell the coffee—you're Amish.

2 out of 5 correct: English is your second language. Maybe third.

3 out of 5 correct: Getting warmer.

4 out of 5 correct: You deserve your own public-access talk show.

5 out of 5 correct: Cheater! Cheater! Cheater!

6 out of 5 correct: Sociopath.

TRUTH *or* TABLOID? can be played alone in an easy chair, with the hospital staff before your anesthetic kicks in, or even in your office cubicle. Can you beat your coworkers?

The boss is betting against you.

TOP
STORIES

A cub reporter will toss in his sleep night after night, praying for that top story to fall from the sky. The career-making scoop that will enable him to move out of Mom and Dad's basement, buy new socks, maybe even afford to date a girl or two, if they're not too demanding.

A seasoned tabloid reporter, like yours truly, will play a round of golf, call in his sports bets, and enjoy a fine lunch of gin and tonic, prime rib, and baked potato, only after which will he show up for work, wrap his arms around the keyboard, and phony up a story or two. Because he knows that getting that juicy top story is easier when it's a do-it-yourself affair. Besides, who can tell the difference? Can you?

GAME 1

Are the following headlines **TRUTH or TABLOID?**
(See next page for correct answers.)

1. **BLIND MAN ACTS AS LOOKOUT IN FAILED ROBBERY ATTEMPT**

2. **ROGER EBERT WILLS SMITHSONIAN HIS THUMBS**

3. **ELECTRONIC BRA PREVENTS BOUNCING BREASTS**

4. **GIRL DIES IN FALL FROM PLATFORM SHOES**

5. **YOU'RE THE REASON OUR KIDS ARE UGLY, CLAIMS EX-WIFE**

1. BLIND MAN ACTS AS LOOKOUT IN FAILED ROBBERY ATTEMPT

TRUTH When Kenneth Bartelson of Pawtucket, Rhode Island, planned a house break-in, he knew he'd need a lookout. Unfortunately, no one except his accomplice Eugene was available, and Eugene is legally blind. No biggie, Kenneth apparently thought. A nearby neighbor called the cops, who arrived to catch the culprits red-handed. Eugene had mistaken the neighbor for Kenneth and was standing next to him when the police drove up.

2. ROGER EBERT WILLS SMITHSONIAN HIS THUMBS

TABLOID "America's attic," in Washington, D.C., has received Archie Bunker's easy chair and many other pop-culture icons, but there are no known plans to exhibit Mr. Ebert's famed thumbs in a pickle jar after he assumes an aisle seat in the great balcony in the sky. Think a popcorn and Coke costs eight dollars in heaven?

3. ELECTRONIC BRA PREVENTS BOUNCING BREASTS

TRUTH In a giant step backward for girl watchers, a Santa Monica, California, inventor has designed an electronic breast-stabilizing brassiere. A two-way switch allows the wearer to stiffen the bra's cups when jogging or engaged in other vigorous activity. Fringe benefit: The electronic wiring also keeps her breasts warm.

4. GIRL DIES IN FALL FROM PLATFORM SHOES

TRUTH Tokyo police investigated the case of a young woman who died tragically when she fell off her seven-inch platform sandals. The towering shoes were a recent fad among many urban Japanese women, who also dyed their hair blond, sported deep tans, and wore micro-mini skirts.

5. YOU'RE THE REASON OUR KIDS ARE UGLY, CLAIMS EX-WIFE

TABLOID Sound like the makings of a good country music song? You're right. "You're the Reason Our Kids Are Ugly" is an old hit tune composed by L. E. White and Lola Dillon.

GAME 2

Are the following headlines **TRUTH *or* TABLOID?**
(See next page for correct answers.)

1. NEW LAW PROTECTS RATS

2. CARDINAL URGES TERM LIMITS FOR POPES

3. MAN ACCUSED OF FAKING OWN DEATH KILLS HIMSELF

4. CHINESE CREATE ARMY OF DEADLY, DISCIPLINED DUCKS

5. CELL PHONE MAKES MAN IMPOTENT

1. NEW LAW PROTECTS RATS

TRUTH Millions of laboratory rats used by United States researchers are now protected under new regulations outlining minimum standards of care. Lab rat to researchers: "First of all, don't call me rat anymore. I'm a research associate. Plus, I get every Sunday off to crawl in the sewer. And I DON'T DO TREADMILLS!"

2. CARDINAL URGES TERM LIMITS FOR POPES

TRUTH In a book, Cardinal Godfried Danneels of Belgium says that there should be a debate on limiting the term of the papacy. One of Europe's most influential cardinals, Danneels feels that the time will soon come when term limits will be expanded from other clergy levels to the papacy itself. A question for Cardinal Danneels: Could you also have this apply to knuckle-rapping Sister X, a certain ruler-wielding grade-school-teaching nun?

3. MAN ACCUSED OF FAKING OWN DEATH KILLS HIMSELF

TABLOID "I can't do anything right!" *Bang!*

4. CHINESE CREATE ARMY OF DEADLY, DISCIPLINED DUCKS

TRUTH Those Commies are at it again. This time, they've trained a so-called elite force of seven hundred thousand ducks to attack on command. What they attack are the locusts that annually plague rural fields. The army is transported to a trouble spot, a whistle is blown, and the "troops" devour every locust in sight. Officials estimate the campaign has cleansed China of a hundred million ethnic locusts. Note: To maintain discipline, any "soldier" who gets out of line is covered with orange sauce, baked, and eaten.

5. CELL PHONE MAKES MAN IMPOTENT

TABLOID Actually, the opposite can happen, according to an Italian consumer group. The association, named Codacons, asked three hundred volunteers to give up their cell phones for fifteen days. One surprising result: About 25 percent reported a dramatic drop in personal confidence that led to sexual problems with their partners.

GAME 3

Are the following headlines **TRUTH *or* TABLOID?**

(See next page for correct answers.)

1. STAR WARS AN OFFICIAL RELIGION

2. BIG BOOBS A BUMMER IN BRAZIL

3. SHOCKING NEW GANGSTA RAP DANCE CRAZE—"THE PRISON STRUT"

4. MOSCOW: DO-IT-YOURSELF POLICE CARS AS LOW AS $1,500

5. TIGER'S ROAR PARALYZES PEOPLE

7

And now, for the CORRECT ANSWERS to GAME 3:

1. STAR WARS AN OFFICIAL RELIGION

TRUTH A recent British census asked citizens to identify their religion. As a prank, or maybe as a protest, an E-mail was circulated urging *Star Wars* fans to list "Jedi" as their belief of choice. Around ten thousand people did just that, forcing the Office for National Statistics to give Jedi an official position on the census form that followed. "When the forms are processed, all data is encoded and we have given 'Jedi Knight' a code because a large group of people have entered it on their forms," said a census official.

2. BIG BOOBS A BUMMER IN BRAZIL

TRUTH In Brazil, large breasts are seen as a libido killer, and breast-reduction surgery is very popular. (Not my libido.)

3. SHOCKING NEW GANGSTA RAP DANCE CRAZE—
THE "PRISON STRUT"

TABLOID Actually, the "prison strut" is cop talk for the swaggering walk characteristic of hardened convicts newly released to the streets. Another con identifier used by savvy police is the "joint body," the big chest and huge arms many prisoners develop by pumping iron. Crime Stopper Tip: If you bump into anyone doing the Prison Strut, turn around and perform the Chicken Run.

4. MOSCOW: DO-IT-YOURSELF POLICE CARS AS LOW AS $1,500

TRUTH In Moscow, a big enough bribe can get just about anything done. Permission to install a flashing police light on your private car runs around $1,500. It's about $400 to obtain a driver's license without a test. Approximately $5,000 to avoid the military draft. And a whopping $100,000 to get a major criminal investigation stopped dead in its tracks.

5. TIGER'S ROAR PARALYZES PEOPLE

TRUTH Scientists at the Fauna Communication Research Institute in North Carolina have discovered that humans can feel as well as hear a tiger's roar, causing a momentary paralysis that may lead to their doom. Describes me to a T when my secretary says, "Phone call from the legal department."

GAME 4

Are the following headlines **TRUTH** *or* **TABLOID?**
(See next page for correct answers.)

1. TEXAS DOC SAYS, "BRAND BABIES TO PREVENT SWITCHING AT BIRTH"

2. BAKED POTATO A TURNING POINT IN HUMAN EVOLUTION

3. GHOSTS FIND COMFORT IN CELL PHONES

4. WOMAN CLAIMS SHE CAUGHT HERPES FROM MANNEQUIN

5. COUPLE CONFESSES SEX CRIME TO 35,000-YEAR-OLD MAN

1. Texas Doc Says, "Brand Babies To Prevent Switching At Birth"

TABLOID Prediction: In the future, branding will replace the tattoo as the body mark of choice. Well, maybe not.

2. Baked Potato A Turning Point In Human Evolution

TRUTH The ability to cook roots like potatoes and carrots was an evolutionary leap forward for our ancestors about 1.9 million years ago, say university anthropologists.

3. Ghosts Find Comfort In Cell Phones

TABLOID Cell phones are actually dangerous to the health of ghosts, according to Tony Cornell of the Society for Psychical Research. The number of ghosts reported to the group has plunged as cell phone use has skyrocketed. Ghost sightings are usually associated with unusual electrical activity in the atmosphere, says Tony, but the electronic "noise" produced by cell phones can overwhelm these otherwordly messages, causing the "death" of ghosts, who can no longer be heard or seen.

4. Woman Claims She Caught Herpes From Mannequin

TRUTH Most female herpes sufferers agree that they got the virus by kissing a dummy. A woman in Hamilton, Indiana, claims to have caught it from practicing mouth-to-mouth resuscitation on a Red Cross mannequin. Shortly after a two-day CPR class, the woman noticed a tingling sensation in her mouth. Her doctor diagnosed oral herpes. The woman filed suit against the Red Cross, claiming the mannequin should've been kept clean with soap and water or chlorine. You should know, though, that the Red Cross does not recommend using chlorine on a first date.

5. Couple Confesses Sex Crime To 35,000-Year-Old Man

TRUTH The couple reportedly revealed their crime to Ramtha, a 35,000-year-old "wise man" channeled by J. Z. Knight. The alleged confession took place before an audience in the state of Washington as Knight channeled Ramtha onstage. I can see the TV movie now: *Ramtha: Crime Buster*. Critics say, "thirty-five-thousand-year-old Ramtha is a criminal's worst nightmare." Costarring Linda Evans; age indeterminate.

GAME 5

Are the following headlines **TRUTH** *or* **TABLOID?**
(See next page for correct answers.)

1. **HIGH-FAT ICE CREAM KILLS MORE PEOPLE THAN GUNS DO**

2. **ARTIFICIAL SPERM WILL END NEED FOR MEN**

3. **DIRE SHORTAGE OF WITNESSES AS EXECUTIONS SKYROCKET**

4. **EMPLOYEE FIRED BECAUSE HE WASN'T MENTALLY DISABLED**

5. **FOR-PROFIT SUICIDE HOTLINE SAVES LIVES AT 65 CENTS A MINUTE**

1. HIGH-FAT ICE CREAM KILLS MORE PEOPLE THAN GUNS DO

TABLOID While it would be interesting to hear an NRA spokesman declaim, "More Americans have been killed by Ben & Jerry's Cherry Garcia than a thousand drive-by shootings," the words have yet to be uttered.

2. ARTIFICIAL SPERM WILL END NEED FOR MEN

TRUTH A combination of chemicals *could* be used as artificial sperm. Doctors at the Institute for Reproductive Medicine and Genetics in Los Angeles recently found a way for the eggs of female mice to reproduce their own chromosomes. Similarities between mice eggs and human eggs mean women may one day have babies without the precious sperm of men. But don't worry, guys. Work has yet to progress beyond the testing of rodents.

3. DIRE SHORTAGE OF WITNESSES AS EXECUTIONS SKYROCKET

TRUTH The rapid pace of United States executions is making it hard to find civilian witnesses, as is required in some states. With an average of six witnesses needed to watch each execution, prison officials are beating the bushes for new blood. Do your civic duty—witness an execution today.

4. EMPLOYEE FIRED BECAUSE HE WASN'T MENTALLY DISABLED

TRUTH William W. of Cleveland, Ohio, filed suit against the Phoenix Society of Cuyahoga County, which offers services to the mentally disabled. Formerly employed there as an office manager, William says he was fired because he was the only employee without a current or previous mental disability. The Phoenix Society claims he simply wasn't doing his job.

Scenario (William to Judge): "I swear my boss flat-out told me, 'You gotta be a nut-job to work around here.'"

5. FOR-PROFIT SUICIDE HOTLINE SAVES LIVES AT 65 CENTS A MINUTE

TABLOID Staffer to caller: "Sir, sir, using vulgarities won't make me one bit more sympathetic to your plight. I repeat—I know you're despondent, but you've got a Visa card that's over the limit already."

GAME 6

Are the following headlines **TRUTH *or* TABLOID?**

(See next page for correct answers.)

1. **PALEONTOLOGISTS NAME NEW DINOSAUR FOR ROCK STAR**

2. **KING ORDERS SUBJECTS NOT TO HAVE SEX**

3. **OFFICE WORKER TURNS CUBICLE INTO DAY-CARE CENTER**

4. **WANT TO INCREASE YOUR IQ? TAKE A SAUNA**

5. **NEW SOFTWARE HELPS DEALERS DISABLE DEADBEATS' VEHICLES**

TRUTH or TABLOID?

1. PALEONTOLOGISTS NAME NEW DINOSAUR FOR ROCK STAR

TRUTH Remember Dire Straits? Their lead guitarist was the talented Mark Knopfler. Scientists who discovered a new dinosaur with long, hooked teeth named it after him. About sixty-five million years old, the remains of the five- to six-foot-long creature were discovered by a research team in Madagascar and officially named *Masiakasaurus knopfleri*.

14

2. KING ORDERS SUBJECTS NOT TO HAVE SEX

TABLOID In truth, the king of Swaziland has vowed not to have sex with his new bride for *five years*. But don't cry for him, Swaziland—he has seven other wives.

3. OFFICE WORKER TURNS CUBICLE INTO DAY-CARE CENTER

TABLOID Most cubicles are cramped enough without adding a sand box and a swing set.

4. WANT TO INCREASE YOUR IQ? TAKE A SAUNA

TABLOID Medical psychologist Dr. Siegfried Lahri of the University of Erlangen-Nurenberg in Germany claims the opposite happens. Says Lehri, "IQ is affected by dehydration, which is why sweating in the sauna can play havoc with your intelligence." It can take the brain more than a day to recover.

5. NEW SOFTWARE HELPS DEALERS DISABLE DEADBEATS' VEHICLES

TRUTH A company called AMS sells the Ontime Payment Protection Device to car dealers. If a customer misses a payment, the ignition can be cut, making it impossible to restart the car without first paying up.

GAME 7

Are the following headlines **TRUTH** *or* **TABLOID**?
(See next page for correct answers.)

1. **THE UNIVERSE MAY TURN INTO JELLY**

2. **IRATE FAMILY SUES OVER EXECUTED INMATE'S LAST MEAL—PIZZA "WITH EVERYTHING" LACKED MEAT**

3. **CURRY MAY PREVENT CANCER**

4. **SEX RESEARCHER UNCOVERS THE CHEATING GENE**

5. **CORPORATE BIGWIG CLAIMS AIR POLLUTION CAUSED BY ANTS**

1. THE UNIVERSE MAY TURN INTO JELLY

TRUTH The universe may be perched on an unstable vacuum and "could suddenly condense into 'jelly,'" according to Dr. Benjamin Allanach of Cern, a particle-physics laboratory based in Geneva, Switzerland. As a result, light would stop shining, electricity would no longer work, and all life forms would disintegrate, BBC News reported. Otherwise, there's nothing to worry about.

2. IRATE FAMILY SUES OVER EXECUTED INMATE'S LAST MEAL—PIZZA "WITH EVERYTHING" LACKED MEAT

TABLOID Domino's Pizza manager to inmate: "Sorry, pal, we no longer guarantee delivery within thirty minutes, even under your circumstances. If the pie arrives cold, put it in your lap and have the executioner turn the chair on low. Should be piping hot in two minutes, tops."

3. CURRY MAY PREVENT CANCER

TRUTH An Indian spice used in curry may help prevent and treat bowel cancer, according to researchers at the British biotech firm Phytopharm. The company's curry cancer pill, dubbed P54, works by inhibiting production of an enzyme involved in certain cancers. In order to cover its bets (perhaps), Phytopharm is also developing P54 as a veterinary product to treat arthritis in dogs. And if *that* doesn't work, the entire batch may find its way to my favorite Indian restaurant as a topping on their scrumptious Streets of Calcutta Doberman Vindaloo.

4. SEX RESEARCHER UNCOVERS THE CHEATING GENE

TABLOID Researchers have not yet been able to find politicians willing to donate DNA for a study.

5. CORPORATE BIGWIG CLAIMS AIR POLLUTION CAUSED BY ANTS

TRUTH Boise Cascade operates a paper mill near Wallula, Washington, where the air quality was judged to contain "excess particulate matter." But a huge ant colony was found near the area's only air-quality monitor. Countless ants swarming over the device skewed the results, according to company spokesman Richard Garber.

GAME 8

Are the following headlines **TRUTH or TABLOID?**
(See next page for correct answers.)

1. ARMY DECLARES WAR ON WITCHES

2. WORTHLESS DOT-COM STOCK CERTIFICATES ARE NOW HIP WALLPAPER

3. DOCTORS REMOVE WOMAN'S HEART TO SAVE IT

4. HIGH-TECH WALLET ALERTS SPOUSE WHEN IT'S OPENED

5. MEIN KAMPF TRANSLATOR BECAME U.S. SENATOR

1. ARMY DECLARES WAR ON WITCHES

TRUTH In a campaign to end witchcraft in northeastern Congo, the Ugandan army, which controlled the area at the time, attacked and killed eight hundred suspected witches. After the "exorcism by bullet" concluded, Major General Odongo Jeje proclaimed, "I have just contacted the officers there, and the situation is calm."

2. WORTHLESS DOT-COM STOCK CERTIFICATES ARE NOW HIP WALLPAPER

TABLOID While the certificates are worth nothing right now, their potential value is growing. In fact, a Pets.com stock certificate, for example, may one day be worth more as a collector's item than it was to Wall Street investors.

Interior decorator to client: "And I recommend the nursery be papered with rose-pink eToys certificates in order to lend the space a delightful child-friendly air."

3. DOCTORS REMOVE WOMAN'S HEART TO SAVE IT

TRUTH Doctors laid the heart in an ice-filled stainless-steel bowl for forty-five minutes before returning it to her chest. Called an autotransplant, the remarkable surgery took place at the Methodist DeBakey Heart Center in Houston. Patient Joanne Minnich, fifty-seven, was suffering from three malignant tumors that couldn't be cut out unless her heart was also removed. She found out about the procedure on the Internet and voluntarily underwent the surgery. Doctors estimated she would have died within two weeks without it.

4. HIGH-TECH WALLET ALERTS SPOUSE WHEN IT'S OPENED

TABLOID Boy, do I wish this was for real, especially around Christmas.

5. MEIN KAMPF TRANSLATOR BECAME U.S. SENATOR

TRUTH Alan Cranston, a former United States senator who died at age eighty-six, was known as a nuclear arms control activist. As a young man, though, he edited the first uncensored English version of Hitler's *Mein Kampf* published in the United States. Ungrateful as ever, Adolf sued him for copyright violation.

GAME 9

Are the following headlines **TRUTH** *or* **TABLOID?**
(See next page for correct answers.)

1. ALABAMA MAN CREATES SUPER CATFISH TO END WORLD HUNGER

2. LAUGHTER IS A LAXATIVE

3. "WEE WILLIES" FORM SMALL-PENIS SUPPORT GROUP

4. BEIJING MAYOR PROMISES TOILET PAPER FOR TOURISTS

5. POISON BOOSTS SEXUAL PROWESS

1. ALABAMA MAN CREATES SUPER CATFISH TO END WORLD HUNGER

TRUTH As any Tennessean can tell you, only in Alabama would a scientist breed a genetically altered catfish to feed the starving masses. Near Auburn, Alabama, Rex Dunham has created a super catfish that grows 50 percent faster than the ordinary sort. Its DNA is mixed with that of carp, salmon, and zebra fish.

2. LAUGHTER IS A LAXATIVE

TABLOID But stop smiling just in case.

3. "WEE WILLIES" FORM SMALL-PENIS SUPPORT GROUP

TABLOID I can just see them gathered in a church meeting room, the smoky air choked with tension and shame. A proud but sad-faced man rises from a gray plastic folding chair: "Hi. My name is Jim . . . and I have a small penis. There. I said it. Men, and you *are* men, don't despair. I'm here to tell you that many Wee Willies have developed healthy social lives and even gone on coffee dates. Unfortunately, there is still too much ignorance in society for us to bear this alone. One day, we too shall march on Washington, D.C. Think of it—a million Wee Willies on the Capitol steps."

4. BEIJING MAYOR PROMISES TOILET PAPER FOR TOURISTS

TRUTH Zhang Mao, mayor of China's capital city, vows to add decadent Western amenities like toilet paper and radios playing "lively music" to public toilets within two years. Vacationers: Until then, you're on your own. What have the local people been using? Mao's *Little Red Book*?

5. POISON BOOSTS SEXUAL PROWESS

TABLOID Don't tell that piece of information to rural Indian men in the Uttar Pradesh vicinity. Many believe that consuming lizard or scorpion poison turns them into round-the-clock studs. Physicians say that such rustic lover boys also experience bleeding from bodily orifices, nerve damage, and breathing problems. It is one of life's great ironies that these side effects are frequently cited as turn-offs by women.

GAME 10

Are the following headlines **TRUTH** *or* **TABLOID?**
(See next page for correct answers.)

1. ONE-ARMED TRUCKER FIGHTS BAN FROM DRIVING

2. SCIENTISTS DISCOVER THEORY TO EVERYTHING

3. GOVERNMENT PLANS TO REMOVE WHITE CELLS FROM OUR BLOOD

4. FALLING IN LOVE IS DEPRESSING TO TEENS

5. OBSESSED WOMAN STALKS HOMER SIMPSON

1. ONE-ARMED TRUCKER FIGHTS BAN FROM DRIVING

TRUTH Scott Cook was a one-armed log-truck driver for eighteen years until ordered to stop by Oregon State Police. Cook claimed he drove better with the stub than with a prosthesis. And, in his defense, he produced a federal permit allowing him to fly a plane with one arm.

2. SCIENTISTS DISCOVER THEORY TO EVERYTHING

TRUTH Famed smart-guy Stephen Hawking claims that the M Theory explains everything. Proponents of the theory contend that there are eleven dimensions and that the sum total of all we know exists in a space and time called a *brane*. For further details, contact Mr. Hawking or that old guy downtown who spends his day yelling at the sun.

3. GOVERNMENT PLANS TO REMOVE WHITE CELLS FROM OUR BLOOD

TRUTH A federal advisory panel recommended that white blood cells be removed from every pint of blood we donate. Why? White blood cells are the primary reason some people suffer fevers and chills after receiving a transfusion. Also, some recipients may be at risk for a virus that hides in white blood cells.

4. FALLING IN LOVE IS DEPRESSING TO TEENS

TRUTH A university study of eighty-two hundred adolescents found that teens involved in romantic relationships were more likely to be depressed than those who were not. This depression is associated with increased levels of delinquency and alcoholism. Reasons for the problems of teen lovers include deteriorating relationships with parents, poorer school performance, and concerns over the end of the romance.

5. OBSESSED WOMAN STALKS HOMER SIMPSON

TABLOID There are, however, numerous documented cases of otherwise normal individuals who see cartoon characters standing *alongside* real friends. Such extraordinary and colorful visions are caused by a neurological condition called the Charles Bonnet Syndrome. On a personal note, I'd like to acknowledge the research assistance provided to me on this answer by my good friend and colleague Rex Morgan, M.D.

LIFESTYLES

The lifestyle section of your newspaper is where you can read about everything from how to conceal drinker's paunch by supersizing your tie to the upcoming seminar at the YMCA on "Tai Chi for Newborns." It's also the part of your newspaper that alerts you to hot new trends like "The Rise of the Postmodern Blintz" and often dubious pop-psych advice from wanna-be Dr. Lauras flailing their arms for your attention. In other words, just about anything goes in the lifestyle section, which can make it hard to separate fact-based headlines from the fictional variety. That's the challenge before you in this chapter's ten thrilling games.

GAME 1

Are the following headlines **TRUTH or TABLOID?**
(See next page for correct answers.)

1. PRETENDING TO CRY AT A FUNERAL IS BAD ETIQUETTE

2. MEN: TO CONCEAL BEER BELLY, WEAR LONG TIE

3. TO WIN A MAN, WOO HIS DOG

4. YOUR BIRTH SIGN DETERMINES WHAT CLOTHES YOU SHOULD WEAR

5. SHY KIDS MORE LIKELY TO HAVE LOUDMOUTH PARENTS

1. PRETENDING TO CRY AT A FUNERAL IS BAD ETIQUETTE

TABLOID It appears that the tears don't have to be sincere, as long as they flow hard and fast. In fact, some experts say that faking your feelings may be the most appropriate way to express support, or at least the one most easily recognized by others.

2. MEN: TO CONCEAL BEER BELLY, WEAR LONG TIE

TRUTH Your tie must reach the top of your belly, says image consultant Ken Karpinski. If it's too short, it will draw attention to your stomach.

3. TO WIN A MAN, WOO HIS DOG

TABLOID Especially when he feeds his Rottweiler better than he feeds you.

4. YOUR BIRTH SIGN DETERMINES WHAT CLOTHES YOU SHOULD WEAR

TRUTH Greg Polkosnik, author of the book *Cosmically Chic*, claims that your birth sign is "intrinsically concerned with your self-expression, and you should not overlook its influence on the way you dress." For example, Gemini women do well in strong colors, mixed patterns, and designers like Karl Lagerfeld. I wonder what birth sign wears Mr. Blackwell's designs.

5. SHY KIDS MORE LIKELY TO HAVE LOUDMOUTH PARENTS

TABLOID Actually, the children of shy parents are more likely to be wallflowers themselves, according to a study of 1,047 children led by Roselind Lieb of the Max Planck Institute of Psychiatry in Germany.

GAME 2

Are the following headlines **TRUTH** *or* **TABLOID?**
(See next page for answers.)

1. NEW "DADDY SADDLE" HELPS KIDS STAY ATOP POP

2. NEW CAR PARKS ITSELF

3. FOR THE MAN WHO HAS EVERYTHING: A TALKING BEER-BOTTLE OPENER

4. TINY VIDEO CAMERA CAN BE SWALLOWED LIKE A PILL

5. CLIENTS DEPRESS HER—SO MASSAGE THERAPIST SUES

1. New "Daddy Saddle" Helps Kids Stay Atop Pop

TRUTH Unfortunately for fathers with bad backs, the Daddy Saddle "features comfy fleece padding and a leather-look seat, plus a hand grip and stirrups for your tyke," according to the Lighter Side catalog, featuring "lighthearted gifts . . . for everyone on your list, since 1914." The Daddy Saddle costs about twenty-three bucks. Warning: not for adult use in compromising situations.

2. New Car Parks Itself

TABLOID Not just yet. However, British designers at Roke Manor Research are working on the problem and may have a product on the market within the decade. Radar will measure the size of the parking space, along with cameras and onboard monitors. Sensors will cause the car to stop automatically if a snoozing vagrant gets in the way.

3. For The Man Who Has Everything: A Talking Beer-Bottle Opener

TRUTH Thirsty? Let the Talking Beer-Bottle Opener speak for you. Each and every time you pop the cap on a tall, cool one, the talking opener shouts out, "Oh, yeah! Time for a beer!" Costs eleven dollars—about the price of a twelve-pack.

4. Tiny Video Camera Can Be Swallowed Like A Pill

TRUTH A company in Israel has created a pill-sized, swallowable capsule that contains a camera, light, and transmitter that produces videos of your digestive tract.

Doc to patient: "Take two aspirin, a video camera, and send me the tape in the morning."

5. Clients Depress Her—So Massage Therapist Sues

TRUTH Carol Vanderpoel, fifty-two, formerly of the Blue Mountain Women's Health Center near Sydney, Australia, received a jury award of $15,600 in damages. The massage therapist claimed she suffered from depression after listening to clients talk about their personal problems.

Client to Carol: "My back aches."

Carol to Client: "Thanks for ruining my day, you whiner."

GAME 3

Are the following headlines **TRUTH** *or* **TABLOID**?
(See next page for correct answers.)

1. To Tell If Your Lover Is Lyin', Smack Him In The Head

2. Typical Mountain Dew Drinker Is Into Bondage

3. Smoking After Sex Banned In Canadian Hotels

4. To Prolong Foreplay, Wear Two Layers Of Clothing

5. Yodelers Make Better Lovers, Swiss Women Report

1. To Tell If Your Lover Is Lyin', Smack Him In The Head

TABLOID Not exactly, but if you hit yourself in the noggin, you might develop the gift. Research does indicate that some brain-injury victims have an amazing ability to detect when someone isn't telling the truth. In an experiment, 73 percent of brain-injury victims could tell when a person was lying, while only 50 percent of others could do likewise. Nancy Etcoff, a psychologist at Massachusetts General Hospital, says that certain brain-injured people, due to their limitations, may be able to detect nuances of facial expression that normal people miss.

2. Typical Mountain Dew Drinker Is Into Bondage

TABLOID While there's no proof to support this headline, I have my suspicions. In fact, on a Yahoo! Mountain Dew fan-club website, a member-in-good-standing reveals his true colors: A warehouse supervisor, he lists his interests as tractors, Web cams, bondage, erotic cartoons, amateurs, and picture trading. Need I say more?

3. Smoking After Sex Banned In Canadian Hotels

TABLOID Don't be ridiculous—people don't have sex in Canadian hotels.

4. To Prolong Foreplay, Wear Two Layers Of Clothing

TABLOID To my knowledge, there's no sex therapist who advocates extending the time of foreplay by wearing two pairs of anything.

5. Yodelers Make Better Lovers, Swiss Women Report

TABLOID And while we're on the subject, neither do the Throat Singers of Tibet. By the way, have those Throat Singers ever had a hit record? Seems like they've been on tour ever since the Chinese burned and pillaged their homeland. You would've thought they'd hit the Top 40 by now. Maybe if they dyed their hair, changed their name to TSOT, and wore flashy outfits instead of those fur hats and floor-length yak coats, they could get a gig opening for Britney Spears. Who's their manager anyway—the Dalai Lama?

GAME 4

Are the following headlines **TRUTH** *or* **TABLOID?**
(See next page for correct answers.)

1. ECCENTRIC DOG LOVERS NAME KIDS "ROVER" AND "SPOT"

2. BLIND MAN HIKES APPALACHIAN TRAIL, FALLS 5,000 TIMES

3. COLLEGE GUYS DEMAND MORE BEER, LESS SEX

4. AUTHOR ADVOCATES TRAINING CHILDREN LIKE DOGS!

5. AUTHOR ADVOCATES TRAINING CHILDREN LIKE CATS!

1. ECCENTRIC DOG LOVERS NAME KIDS "ROVER" AND "SPOT"

TABLOID My parents just whistled.

2. BLIND MAN HIKES APPALACHIAN TRAIL, FALLS 5,000 TIMES

TRUTH Incredibly, a blind man named Bill Irwin hiked the rugged trail from Georgia to Maine with just his Seeing Eye dog to guide him. Only a small percentage of people who attempt the arduous twenty-one-hundred-mile trek complete it. Mr. Irwin estimated that he fell down on five thousand separate occasions—more than two times per mile!

3. COLLEGE GUYS DEMAND MORE BEER, LESS SEX

TABLOID Rest easy, college girls. Even though it may sometimes seem that nothing comes between your beau and his beer keg, sex is always first and foremost on his mind. With you, of course.

4. AUTHOR ADVOCATES TRAINING CHILDREN LIKE DOGS!

TRUTH Former high-school teacher Harold Hansen has been training dogs for twenty-two years. When he became a stepfather, he began to apply his dog-training techniques in his home life, with rewarding results. That's what he claims in his book *The Dog Trainer's Guide to Parenting*.

5. AUTHOR ADVOCATES TRAINING CHILDREN LIKE CATS!

TABLOID Are you outta your mind? What kinda kook would recommend treating your kid like a house pet?

GAME 5

Are the following headlines **TRUTH** *or* **TABLOID**?
(See next page for correct answers.)

1. **DRUNKS MAKE BETTER PUBLIC SPEAKERS**

2. **TO PICK UP MORE WOMEN, SAY "I'M GOING TO ANTARCTICA"**

3. **GUYS: TO TELL IF YOU'RE GONNA "SCORE," STARE AT HER FOREHEAD**

4. **BERSERK BRIDES-TO-BE BURGLARIZE BRIDAL BOUTIQUE**

5. **POLYGAMIST DIVORCES 2 WIVES, MARRIES 3, FOR NET GAIN OF 1**

1. DRUNKS MAKE BETTER PUBLIC SPEAKERS

TRUTH Researchers at the University of Michigan found that just the thought of being intoxicated relaxed public speakers. Maybe that's why some politicians never seem to make sense.

2. TO PICK UP MORE WOMEN, SAY "I'M GOING TO ANTARCTICA"

TRUTH That's according to a textbook on Antarctic psychology published by Victoria University in New Zealand. In a study, two men placed a personal ad in a magazine asking for "active female companionship for a week for fit men about to go to the Antarctic." They were overwhelmed with offers. Anecdotal reports from New Zealand also agree that men who claim they are about to leave for the Antarctic have great success with women.

3. GUYS: TO TELL IF YOU'RE GONNA "SCORE," STARE AT HER FOREHEAD

TRUTH Researcher Calin Prodan of the University of Oklahoma Health Sciences Center showed line drawings displaying different emotions on the upper and lower portions of a human face to twenty subjects. Most people focused on the nose, lips, and cheeks, even though the true emotions were being expressed by the eyes, brows, and forehead. Which means that in noisy environments, like a bar, a guy will focus on a girl's lips to understand what she's saying. He'd be better off staring at her forehead to discover what she's really feeling.

4. BERSERK BRIDES-TO-BE BURGLARIZE BRIDAL BOUTIQUE

TRUTH When the Bridal Designs store in Los Angeles closed for a weekend, dozens of angry women panicked. Believing the boutique was going out of business, several brides-to-be broke in to save their gowns from the auction block. Thankfully, it was all a big mistake, according to store owner Bruce Anderson. An employee shortage had forced the weekend closure, not bankruptcy. When the boutique reopened, several relieved customers helped Anderson assist shoppers.

5. POLYGAMIST DIVORCES 2 WIVES, MARRIES 3, FOR NET GAIN OF 1

TABLOID Polygamists don't keep score. I think.

GAME 6

Are the following headlines **TRUTH** or **TABLOID**?
(See next page for correct answers.)

1. **CLOWNS CAUSE TERMINALLY ILL TO DIE FASTER**

2. **SHRINK TREATS PATIENTS WITH $150 PER HOUR "CLOWN THERAPY"**

3. **TO IMPROVE ROMANTIC RELATIONSHIP, WET YOUR PANTS**

4. **LAUGHTER THERAPIST CONCLUDES "CLOWNS ARE DOWNERS"**

5. **TO EASE PAIN OF CHILDBIRTH, OB/GYN DOC TELLS JOKES**

1. CLOWNS CAUSE TERMINALLY ILL TO DIE FASTER

TABLOID Sorry, clown haters. A $150,000 study commissioned by the Rosenthal Center for Complementary and Alternative Medicine found that clowns actually offer benefits to terminal and other patients. To quote from one finding of the three-part study: "The research efforts were successful in that Critical Care Unit clowns were introduced into three medical settings in which they had no prior experience, and have remained there even after completion of the studies. Not only did they help us demonstrate the feasibility of introducing clowns into settings where painful, invasive procedures are performed, they also showed how their very presence transforms the expectations of caregivers and patients alike."

2. SHRINK TREATS PATIENTS WITH $150 PER HOUR "CLOWN THERAPY"

TABLOID I didn't find any psychoanalysts who've exchanged their cherished Rorschach inkblot collections for fright wigs, but there are many clown-therapy enthusiasts, as revealed in this notice about Rochester General Hospital: "Hugh Brown, better known as 'Shuffles,' was once a patient here. Now he's prescribing doses of laughter to those who need a pick-me-up."

3. TO IMPROVE ROMANTIC RELATIONSHIP, WET YOUR PANTS

TRUTH Laughter therapist Enda Junkins, LMSW, has twenty essential "Laughter Tips for Relationships" on her website. Among them is a suggestion to "practice laughing without control. Spit out food, wet your pants, wet each other's pants." Be sure to wear your Depends.

4. LAUGHTER THERAPIST CONCLUDES "CLOWNS ARE DOWNERS"

TABLOID There isn't a laughter therapist worth her salt who doesn't believe in the healing power of clowns. "Equally important," says the Rosenthal study, "positive changes in the behavior and mood of hospital caregivers were observed when the clowns were around."

5. TO EASE PAIN OF CHILDBIRTH, OB/GYN DOC TELLS JOKES

TABLOID Doc: "Have I told you the one about the time a fly got in my soup?" Patient: "Yes, two babies ago."

GAME 7

Are the following headlines **TRUTH** *or* **TABLOID?**
(See next page for correct answers.)

1. **COLLECTOR WEARS SAME T-SHIRT FOR TEN YEARS**

2. **U.S. SENATOR ADMIRES FEMALE DUMMIES**

3. **HARVARD JET WHISKS SELECT STUDENTS HOME FOR HOLIDAYS**

4. **RECYCLED LINT BECOMES SWEATERS FOR HIP**

5. **WIFE SWAPPING WAS INVENTED IN 1957**

1. COLLECTOR WEARS SAME T-SHIRT FOR TEN YEARS

TABLOID Actually, collector Waldo Stuart of Phoenix owns more than four thousand T-shirts. Wearing one a day, he could go for ten years without repeating. And T-shirts must run in the Stuart blood because Waldo's thirteen-year-old daughter already has a thousand.

2. U.S. SENATOR ADMIRES FEMALE DUMMIES

TRUTH Senator Barbara Boxer of California has announced her support of female dummies—crash-test variety. Senator Boxer, who is barely five feet tall herself, believes that smaller-sized dummies should be used in government-mandated crash tests to duplicate better how women are affected in accidents. Currently, all dummies are a man-sized five feet eight inches tall and 172 pounds. Boxer advocates that a four-feet-eleven-inch, 108-pound "female" dummy be included in all tests.

3. HARVARD JET WHISKS SELECT STUDENTS HOME FOR HOLIDAYS

TABLOID If Harvard has one, famed law professor Alan Dershowitz probably hogs it . . . or that psychology professor who believes alien abductions are real.

4. RECYCLED LINT BECOMES SWEATERS FOR HIP

TABLOID Just a thought that came to mind when removing an extra-large handful of stuff from my lint filter. In fact, some people believe clothes dryers are a slow way of killing off your favorite garments, as they gradually remove the fabric's fibers.

5. WIFE SWAPPING WAS INVENTED IN 1957

TRUTH Apparently, it was autumn 1957 when the first article featuring the precise term "wife swapping" was published in *Mr.*, a Manhattan-based men's magazine. The publication featured a short article on the topic, along with lots of photos of busty, seminude women. The newly coined term took off like a rocket, showing up in other quality publications of the era, like *Hush-Hush, True Divorce, True Weird,* and *Rave.*

GAME 8

Are the following headlines **TRUTH** *or* **TABLOID?**
(See next page for correct answers.)

1. **DRIVERS CAMP OUT FOR WEEKS IN WORST TRAFFIC JAM EVER**

2. **DEATH ROW KILLERS DENIED COMPUTER ACCESS**

3. **WOMAN EARNS LIVING AS PROFESSIONAL SKIPPER**

4. **MAD COW DISEASE FORCES CLOSURE OF S&M "LEATHER BAR"**

5. **POLICEWOMEN TALK DIRTY THE BEST**

1. DRIVERS CAMP OUT FOR WEEKS IN WORST TRAFFIC JAM EVER

TRUTH Twenty years ago, the main highway in the Congo was asphalt-paved and took two hours to drive. Now the 170-mile trip can last up to an incredible two months! War and neglect have turned the Kinshasa-Matadi road into a bombed-out quagmire where thousands of vehicles are often stranded at once. Villagers along the route earn extra money providing food to travelers who camp out while waiting for assistance in moving. Yet, truckers continue long after their cargo has spoiled—to prove to their bosses that they didn't sell it along the way.

2. DEATH ROW KILLERS DENIED COMPUTER ACCESS

TABLOID In fact, all inmates on Maryland's death row now have computer access. Many sit in front of the screen for hours each day, researching their cases on legal-reference software. Prison officials say the arrangement is no different than allowing access to law books, but victims' rights groups express outrage.

3. WOMAN EARNS LIVING AS PROFESSIONAL SKIPPER

TRUTH Kim Corbin of San Francisco lost twenty-five pounds by skipping—instead of walking—on errands. Now she receives funding from a fitness organization to spread the word about better health through skipping. Kim is often seen skipping in Golden Gate Park on weekends, encouraging others to join along.

4. MAD COW DISEASE FORCES CLOSURE OF S&M "LEATHER BAR"

TABLOID An earlier outbreak of the disease led to a shortage of leather for Nike athletic shoes. Will whips and leather pants be the next to go?

5. POLICEWOMEN TALK DIRTY THE BEST

TABLOID It's the *wives* of policemen who talk dirty the best, according to one of Europe's biggest phone-sex providers. In fact, the company hires only cops' wives because of their extraordinary enthusiasm for red-hot sex talk.

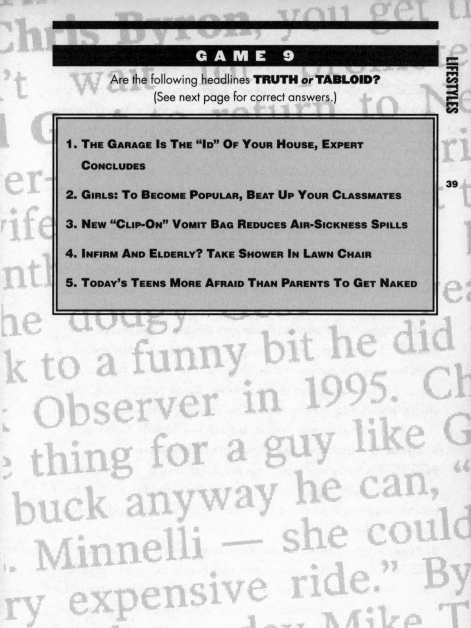

GAME 9

Are the following headlines **TRUTH *or* TABLOID?**
(See next page for correct answers.)

1. THE GARAGE IS THE "ID" OF YOUR HOUSE, EXPERT CONCLUDES

2. GIRLS: TO BECOME POPULAR, BEAT UP YOUR CLASSMATES

3. NEW "CLIP-ON" VOMIT BAG REDUCES AIR-SICKNESS SPILLS

4. INFIRM AND ELDERLY? TAKE SHOWER IN LAWN CHAIR

5. TODAY'S TEENS MORE AFRAID THAN PARENTS TO GET NAKED

1. THE GARAGE IS THE "ID" OF YOUR HOUSE, EXPERT CONCLUDES

TRUTH According to psychoanalytic theory, the id is the part of the psyche that is completely unconscious; it's the source of psychic energy derived from instinctual needs and drives. "I call [the garage] the id, the id of the house. It really is," Kira Obolensky told an interviewer for the Knight-Ridder News Service. Obolensky is the author of *Garage: Reinventing the Place We Park*. No mention was made of what rooms the ego and superego occupy or where to store the id when you live in an apartment.

2. GIRLS: TO BECOME POPULAR, BEAT UP YOUR CLASSMATES

TABLOID Actually, this tip works only for boys. Psychologists who studied children in fifty-nine classrooms found that aggressive, antisocial boys in the fourth, fifth, and sixth grades often became the most socially connected. Their fellow (obviously wimpy) students saw them as cool and athletic.

3. NEW "CLIP-ON" VOMIT BAG REDUCES AIR-SICKNESS SPILLS

TABLOID Some things never change, like the classic airline vomit bag. More than one has become a collectible, but not in the way that you think. Fans of barf bags trade them over the Internet, like baseball cards or Pamela Lee Anderson wedding-night videos. One fifteen-year-old, who calls himself "Tak," owns 175 vomit bags, including the elusive Estonian Air model.

4. INFIRM AND ELDERLY? TAKE SHOWER IN LAWN CHAIR

TRUTH A home-care expert says that if Grandma is weak and feeble, unfold a lawn chair in the shower so that she may bathe. Place a bath towel beneath so that it doesn't slip. Hey, don't grumble! He could've recommended a La-Z-Boy recliner.

5. TODAY'S TEENS MORE AFRAID THAN PARENTS TO GET NAKED

TRUTH Despite the risqué videos and bawdy rap lyrics that assault them, today's kids are more reluctant to reveal their naked bodies in locker rooms and such than baby boomers were at the same age—or are now. That's the word from Neil Howe and William Strauss, coauthors of a book on adolescents titled *Millennials Rising*.

GAME 10

Are the following headlines **TRUTH** *or* **TABLOID?**
(See next page for correct answers.)

1. TINY DACHSHUND IS WURST GAS-PASSING PUP

2. SCHOOLBOY INSANE FROM CIGARETTES!

3. HEALTH-CONSCIOUS L.A. SUFFERS SHORTAGE OF LARD

4. NOW YOU TOO CAN OWN THE WORLD'S SMARTEST FORK!

5. GHOSTS FOUND IN TOILET

1. TINY DACHSHUND IS WURST GAS-PASSING PUP

TABLOID The German shepherd takes the prize, according to a survey of dog owners conducted for CurTail, a canine antiflatulence product. Why German shepherds pass more gas is unknown to veterinary science. Maybe it's because these *horribly savage beasts* have trouble digesting the raw flesh of the human leg. (Obviously, my encounters with German shepherds have not been happy.)

2. SCHOOLBOY INSANE FROM CIGARETTES!

TABLOID But this is a real newspaper headline from the early-twentieth-century period of "yellow" journalism, proving that people loved tabloids even before Elizabeth Taylor and Michael Jackson were born.

3. HEALTH-CONSCIOUS L.A. SUFFERS SHORTAGE OF LARD

TRUTH The home of sprouts and Calista Flockhart suffered another blow to its image awhile back. The widespread popularity of Mexican food, which in its authentic form is heavy on lard, caused a shortage of the melted pig fat at local processors. The Farmer John factory in downtown L.A. was slaughtering six to seven thousand hogs *a day*, yet lard-hungry customers had to be turned away due to voracious demand.

4. NOW YOU TOO CAN OWN THE WORLD'S SMARTEST FORK!

TRUTH A half-page ad in trustworthy, seventeen-million-circulation *Parade* magazine offered "The World's Smartest Fork" for only $9.98. The "professional chef's Sensor Fork with built-in thermometer ends undercooking or overcooking ONCE AND FOR ALL!" Featuring the high-tech gizmo's LCD window, the ad also emphasized that "BATTERIES ARE INCLUDED!" A price break allowed readers to order three forks for only $24.98.

5. GHOSTS FOUND IN TOILET

TABLOID There is, though, a Korean folk myth that has long held that evil ghosts lurk in outhouse holes. Rustic believers clear their throats before stepping into the family outhouse, in order to "spook" the spirits, and if by some chance a child topples into the depths, complimentary rice cakes are offered for the entities to eat instead.

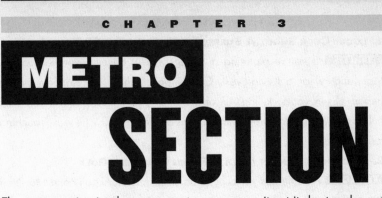

CHAPTER 3

METRO SECTION

The metro section is where you meet your community at its best and worst. Where else can you read, as you sip your morning coffee, about sensitivity-trained tree trimmers or the grade school that slaughtered its pet steer for educational purposes? Moreover, how about that wonderful semiretired whittler's hand-carved popsicle sticks? And let's not forget those metro section stalwarts—the bumbling criminals who make the police blotter zing. In fact, there are enough true oddballs in every town to make separating truth from fiction tricky. Test your skills on these headlines.

GAME 1

Are the following headlines **TRUTH** *or* **TABLOID?**
(See next page for correct answers.)

1. **LOCAL COPS SHOOT A SUSPECT A MONTH—FOR 10 YEARS!**

2. **NEIGHBORS AGHAST OVER X-RATED MINIATURE GOLF**

3. **HOW HOT IS IT? FROZEN DINNER COOKS ON CAR SEAT!**

4. **OVEREAGER TEEN LAUNCHES 2020 PRESIDENTIAL BID**

5. **ANIMAL CRACKER–SHAPED HAILSTONES PUMMEL TEXAS TOWN**

And now, for the CORRECT ANSWERS to GAME 1:

1. LOCAL COPS SHOOT A SUSPECT A MONTH—FOR 10 YEARS!

TRUTH If you're planning a crime spree in Prince George's County, Maryland, wear a Kevlar vest. County police shot 122 suspects over a period of ten years, killing 47 of them. One unarmed truck driver, who pulled off the road to relieve himself, was blasted because he was "reaching for his pants."

2. NEIGHBORS AGHAST OVER X-RATED MINIATURE GOLF

TABLOID No one has yet to build an erotic miniature golf course to see if they will come.

3. HOW HOT IS IT? FROZEN DINNER COOKS ON CAR SEAT!

TRUTH In a mind-frying experiment, a TV station in Phoenix, Arizona, placed a frozen dinner in a locked car with the windows rolled up under the broiling afternoon sun. The air temperature was 120 degrees. Inside the much-hotter car, the dinner cooked to perfection.

4. OVEREAGER TEEN LAUNCHES 2020 PRESIDENTIAL BID

TRUTH James Williams of Portland, Oregon, is nothing if not ambitious. At the age of seventeen, he set up a website in order to mount a serious bid for a 2020 presidential run. Williams, who usually wears a dark suit and tie, was a representative to the Portland School Board at sixteen, only the second student to be so honored in the board's history. "For a long time, I've wanted to become president," says Williams. "This desire has only grown stronger as I have seen politics played out at the state, local, and national levels."

5. ANIMAL CRACKER–SHAPED HAILSTONES PUMMEL TEXAS TOWN

TABLOID But hailstones shaped like baseballs, footballs, hickory nuts, grapefruits, coffee cups, miniature trolls, and pennies have been reported all over the United States. And cricket ball–sized hailstones killed one person and injured thirty during a violent storm in eastern Australia.

GAME 2

Are the following headlines **TRUTH or TABLOID?**
(See next page for correct answers.)

1. MILITANT NUDE SUNBATHERS THREATEN WOMAN

2. MOM SUES NEIGHBOR FOR TELLING KIDS SANTA'S NOT REAL

3. HICCUPING MAN KILLED BY PUNCH MEANT TO HELP

4. STOLEN CAR STOLEN AGAIN BEFORE RETURN TO OWNER

5. DOMINO'S DRIVER CAUGHT SPRINKLING "MAGIC MUSHROOMS"
   ON PIZZAS

1. MILITANT NUDE SUNBATHERS THREATEN WOMAN

TRUTH So claims Teri Powers, a resident of Portland, Oregon. In a courtroom appearance, Powers said that nudists destroyed signs, demolished gates, and threatened to burn her beachfront house to the ground. They also warned that they were "organized and militant," which made Powers and her family feel like prisoners in their own home. Surely, there is no greater fear than facing down a menacing band of sunburned nudists.

2. MOM SUES NEIGHBOR FOR TELLING KIDS SANTA'S NOT REAL

TABLOID No self-respecting adult would ever burst a child's bubble and reveal that Santa's an out-and-out fake . . . and that her mom and dad are behind an enormous cover-up. "They hide the presents in the attic and put them under the tree after you go to sleep. Dad eats the cookies and milk and mom's consulting a therapist because the lies are eating her up. Their marriage is in trouble and it's all your fault because of your selfish need to believe in Santa Claus."

3. HICCUPING MAN KILLED BY PUNCH MEANT TO HELP

TRUTH In Ocean City, Maryland, a guy named Joshua Burchette, age twenty-three, couldn't get rid of the hiccups, so he asked a friend to punch him in the chest. The friend complied and Joshua died on the spot. His mother said the family had a history of heart problems.

4. STOLEN CAR STOLEN AGAIN BEFORE RETURN TO OWNER

TRUTH One fine Renton, Washington, morning, Ken Kramer's 1992 Ford Explorer was stolen. The cops found it downtown a few days later, but by the time Ken showed up to claim it four hours after he was notified, his SUV had been stolen again. Said an astonished Ken, "I could not even make this up."

5. DOMINO'S DRIVER CAUGHT SPRINKLING "MAGIC MUSHROOMS" ON PIZZAS

TABLOID The only magic is when you can *find* a mushroom on one of their pizzas. Just kidding, Domino's lawyers!

GAME 3

Are the following headlines **TRUTH** *or* **TABLOID?**
(See next page for correct answers.)

1. IF YOU WANT TO GET MURDERED, STAY HOME SATURDAY NIGHT

2. JUDGE SUSPENDED FOR THROWING ROCKS

3. CAFFEINE POLLUTES OCEAN NEAR STARBUCKS'S HOMETOWN

4. WOMAN GIVES BIRTH IN TAXI; CABBIE INSISTS ON $257.98 FARE

5. MAN JAILED FOR YAWNING

1. IF YOU WANT TO GET MURDERED, STAY HOME SATURDAY NIGHT

TRUTH Most murders occur as the result of a domestic dispute between the hours of 6 P.M. Saturday and 6 P.M. Sunday. And the deadliest days are Christmas Eve and New Year's Eve. Crime Stopper Tip: Lower the murder rate in your living room by working weekends and holidays.

2. JUDGE SUSPENDED FOR THROWING ROCKS

TRUTH Late in 2001, Metro Judge Barbara Brown of Albuquerque, New Mexico, was temporarily suspended after the police charged her with throwing rocks at a check-cashing store. Allegedly, a clerk had refused to grant the judge a new loan because she had not yet paid off a prior one.

3. CAFFEINE POLLUTES OCEAN NEAR STARBUCKS'S HOMETOWN

TRUTH Scientists in Seattle were planning to use caffeine as a "marker" to identify leaking sewer pipes and other sources of human waste flowing untreated into the sound. But the waters surrounding Seattle were already polluted by caffeine, which rendered their equipment ineffective. Why? Caffeine doesn't break down on its quick journey in and out of the body. Plus, Seattle espresso-cart vendors and motorists were in the habit of pouring their cold leftovers into storm drains.

4. WOMAN GIVES BIRTH IN TAXI; CABBIE INSISTS ON $257.98 FARE

TABLOID "Listen, lady, this ain't no hospital. The meter's been runnin' three hours."

5. MAN JAILED FOR YAWNING

TRUTH In Eugene, Oregon, twenty-year-old Nick Patrick Steece was slapped with a twenty-day sentence by Circuit Judge Ted Carp for yawning during an arraignment in court. Bet that woke him up.

GAME 4

Are the following headlines **TRUTH or TABLOID?**
(See next page for correct answers.)

1. Edgy Wax Museum Allows Visitors To Melt Figures

2. Blind Woman Guided By Seeing Eye Horse

3. Autopsy Performed On Teddy Bear

4. A City So Poor, Its Police Cars Were Repossessed

5. A City So Poor, Its Fire Truck Used A Garden Hose

1. EDGY WAX MUSEUM ALLOWS VISITORS TO MELT FIGURES

TABLOID Wouldn't it be fun to blowtorch the wax nose of your least-favorite celebrity? But wax museums are pretty much a dying breed. One all-time favorite is the Criminals' Hall of Fame Wax Museum on the Ontario side of Niagra Falls. Hitler had been a featured exhibit, but apparently someone stole his uniform awhile back.

2. BLIND WOMAN GUIDED BY SEEING EYE HORSE

TRUTH Cricket, a twenty-six-inch, seventy-pound miniature horse, leads Cheryle King of Gig Harbor, Washington, through her daily routine. Cricket went through eight months of rigorous training before moving in with her new owner, who lost her eyesight to multiple sclerosis. Experts say miniature horses have a wide field of vision and can live twenty to thirty years longer than dogs.

3. AUTOPSY PERFORMED ON TEDDY BEAR

TABLOID The procedure has yet to show up in the annals of medicine—or on the 325,000 websites devoted to teddy bears, at least one of which sells bears with mink fur.

4. A CITY SO POOR, ITS POLICE CARS WERE REPOSSESSED

TRUTH In the 1970s, the city of Benton Harbor, Michigan (population 9,000), was in such deep financial trouble that its five police cars were repossessed. Officers resorted to driving cars belonging to the building inspection department.

Building inspector to cop: "There's a front porch I need you to check out on your way to the crime scene."

5. A CITY SO POOR, ITS FIRE TRUCK USED A GARDEN HOSE

TRUTH Once again Benton Harbor's money problems forced it to extreme measures for a while in the seventies. The western Michigan city's one and only pumper truck had just a garden hose with which to spray water on fires.

Fire chief to wife: "Honey, could I borrow the hose for an hour? There's a four-alarm fire downtown."

GAME 5

Are the following headlines **TRUTH _or_ TABLOID?**
(See next page for correct answers.)

1. **Family Destroys Life-Threatening Home**

2. **Fed-Up Kids Tell Wild Parents They're Grounded**

3. **Inner-City Traffic Cops Target Suburban Soccer Moms**

4. **Stupid Bank Promotion: Deposit Bucks, Get A Gun**

5. **Principal Asks Female Students To Wear Tube Tops**

1. FAMILY DESTROYS LIFE-THREATENING HOME

TRUTH This is not a Stephen King haunted-house tale. Mark and Mary Jane O'Hara of Eugene, Oregon, believed that a 1998 remodeling job had caused their home to become infested with mold and blamed the mold for a series of health problems that plagued family members. For instance, Mark, a dentist, was once hospitalized with inflamed sinuses after spending just a few minutes at home, even though he was wearing protective gear. Disgusted, the O'Haras allowed the local fire department to burn the house down in a practice exercise.

2. FED-UP KIDS TELL WILD PARENTS THEY'RE GROUNDED

TABLOID Do kids really care if their parents ever come home, except to make dinner and replace the batteries in their cell phones?

3. INNER-CITY TRAFFIC COPS TARGET SUBURBAN SOCCER MOMS

TABLOID Traffic officers are not profiling SUVs driven by mothers under the influence of cell phones. Unfortunately.

4. STUPID BANK PROMOTION: DEPOSIT BUCKS, GET A GUN

TRUTH During a promotion at the North Country Bank and Trust in Traverse City, Michigan, buying a two-thousand-dollar twenty-year CD earned you a 12-gauge shotgun or a .270-caliber hunting rifle. You didn't even have to be a Michigan resident to take part. Fringe benefit: All firearms were highly coveted Weatherbys, which—like Ferraris—rise in value over time.

5. PRINCIPAL ASKS FEMALE STUDENTS TO WEAR TUBE TOPS

TABLOID The boys weren't asked to wear muscle shirts, either.

GAME 6

Are the following headlines **TRUTH or TABLOID?**

(See next page for correct answers.)

1. **Bus Driver Fired For Drag Racing To Impress Girlfriend**

2. **Kick-Off Of Amputee Soccer Tournament Announced**

3. **Officials O.K. Killing Angry Pigs**

4. **Tattoo Artists Ink 1,000 Butts For Charity**

5. **Rainbows Promote Homosexuality, Say Citizens**

And now, for the CORRECT ANSWERS to GAME 6:

1. Bus Driver Fired For Drag Racing To Impress Girlfriend

TABLOID Bus driver: "Watch me beat that street sweeper off the line."

Girlfriend: "I love a man who makes me grip the strap tight."

2. Kick-Off Of Amputee Soccer Tournament Announced

TRUTH Amputee soccer began twenty years ago in Seattle, when Donald Bennett, now in his seventies, invited other soccer devotees who'd lost a leg to start a league. Recently, the World Cup Amputee Soccer Tournament returned to Seattle to kick off an international competition. Players move about the field on crutches, using their good leg to kick the ball. Goalies may possess both legs but must be missing a hand or an arm.

3. Officials O.K. Killing Angry Pigs

TRUTH The trapping and killing of aggressive pigs won the approval of the Oregon Department of Agriculture. The wild, angry pigs were believed to be the offspring of hogs that had escaped from ranches to occupy 520 square miles of territory, with the potential to double in population every four months.

4. Tattoo Artists Ink 1,000 Butts For Charity

TABLOID The tattooing community has yet to band together for such a noble endeavor.

5. Rainbows Promote Homosexuality, Say Citizens

TRUTH The rainbows in question were on bumper stickers affixed to police cars in Traverse City, Michigan. Overlaid with human figures, the stickers were meant to promote diversity, according to city officials. But a campaign of hundreds of E-mails and letters from archconservatives claimed the rainbow emblem was a symbol of acceptance for gays. In order to quiet the outcry, the Traverse City Commission agreed to remove the bumper stickers from all government vehicles. So much for equality.

GAME 7

Are the following headlines **TRUTH** *or* **TABLOID?**
(See next page for correct answers.)

1. **TEACHER ASSAULTS STUDENT WITH PLAY-DOH**

2. **STEER SLAUGHTERED TO TEACH KIDS WHERE STEAKS COME FROM**

3. **MAN CONVICTED FOR SEX WITH 28-YEAR-OLD MINOR**

4. **PSYCHO FILLED DEAD BODY WITH SAVORY STUFFING**

5. **FIRST DRIVE-BY SHOOTING FROM MOTORIZED SCOOTER**

1. TEACHER ASSAULTS STUDENT WITH PLAY-DOH

TABLOID But seventy-year-old Doris Galewick, a kindergarten teacher at Shasta Meadows Elementary School in Redding, California, allegedly poked one of her students twenty times with a toothpick. Why? To teach *him* not to do the same to his classmates.

2. STEER SLAUGHTERED TO TEACH KIDS WHERE STEAKS COME FROM

TRUTH Students as young as five at Carbon Canyon Christian School in California observed the killing and slaughtering of a half-ton bull in order to teach them where meat comes from. The two-year-old steer, nicknamed T-Bone, had been raised at the school. About half of the school's 170 students watched as a butcher killed and skinned the animal, then removed its organs to show them. "It was an awesome experience," said principal Dave Kincer. "It gave them a chance to see up close what they've been reading about in books all year."

Student to mother: "Look what we did in school today, Mommy!"

Mother to student: "That's a bag full of steaks!"

3. MAN CONVICTED FOR SEX WITH 28-YEAR-OLD MINOR

TRUTH Bear with me on this one, because the details are pretty involved. Treva Thronberry, thirty-one, was arrested on charges of first- and second-degree theft and perjury. She was allegedly pretending to be an eighteen-year-old student at Clark College in the state of Washington and had been enrolled in high school for three years before that, beginning in 1997. In 1998, Charles Blankenship, then forty-four, pleaded guilty to communicating with a minor for immoral purposes. The "minor," who authorities then believed to be age sixteen, was really twenty-eight. When her true age was discovered, Blankenship was cleared of all charges.

4. PSYCHO FILLED DEAD BODY WITH SAVORY STUFFING

TABLOID Even Norman Bates would have disapproved.

5. FIRST DRIVE-BY SHOOTING FROM MOTORIZED SCOOTER

TABLOID Given how many pedestrians those scooters irritate, it's the driver of one of them who's likely to get blasted first.

GAME 8

Are the following headlines **TRUTH** *or* **TABLOID**?
(See next page for correct answers.)

1. **LOCAL MAN EARNS LIVING BY SLEEPING**

2. **TOWN NAMES NEW STREET "GARBAGE ROAD"**

3. **CAT BURGLAR USES WHEELCHAIR**

4. **FLORIDA TREE TRIMMERS GET SENSITIVITY TRAINING**

5. **BBQ CHAMP CURES MEAT WITH MARIJUANA**

1. LOCAL MAN EARNS LIVING BY SLEEPING

TABLOID Tim Nelson of Dayton, Tennessee, does have a job testing La-Z-Boy recliners as they come off the assembly line. Tim reclines in more than one hundred chairs a day to test the quality of their build. However, unlike most La-Z-Boy users, he's not allowed to sleep, watch football, or drink beer.

2. TOWN NAMES NEW STREET "GARBAGE ROAD"

TRUTH The city of Florence, Oregon, named a new street Garbage Road, which caused an outraged citizen to write to the local paper, "It is hard to believe that we paid a county worker to dream up this name, paid to have the sign made, then paid to have it installed." R-e-ev-ol—ution now!!

3. CAT BURGLAR USES WHEELCHAIR

TABLOID Although disabled people are capable of many feats, one has yet to commit second-story burglary.

4. FLORIDA TREE TRIMMERS GET SENSITIVITY TRAINING

TRUTH No, they didn't learn how to avoid hurting the feelings of branches and twigs. This was all about the owners of property upon which trees lived. In a move to eliminate a bacterial infection, crews were invading residential neighborhoods and chopping down trees with barely a warning to the people who lived there. So, in order to be more sympathetic, the tree trimmers were ordered to attend a two-day sensitivity training seminar before returning to work.

5. BBQ CHAMP CURES MEAT WITH MARIJUANA

TABLOID While pork ribs have yet to be seasoned with pot, it looks like secondhand exposure to marijuana can cause unexpected problems. In England, a former police detective was compensated for a habit he picked up after handling too much marijuana in the evidence room—snoring loudly every night.

GAME 9

Are the following headlines **TRUTH** *or* **TABLOID**?
(See next page for correct answers.)

1. **Homeless Applaud Politically Correct Garbage Cans**

2. **Resort Community Features Combat Obstacle Course**

3. **Barfly Finds "Happy Hour" Depressing**

4. **Cars Average 190 MPH On Country Road**

5. **Beauty Queen Dethroned For Being Too Thin**

1. Homeless Applaud Politically Correct Garbage Cans

TRUTH The city of Portland, Oregon, commissioned the firm of ZIBA Design to create a garbage can that would allow the homeless to retrieve empty bottles and cans without diving through the rest of the trash. Dubbed "politically correct," the new stainless-steel design features an attached bin for drink containers, which fetch ten cents apiece when returned to recycling centers. The new trash cans sell for $870 each, and Portland ordered one hundred of them.

2. Resort Community Features Combat Obstacle Course

TRUTH About $300,000 buys you a one-acre home site at Front Sight, an exclusive $25-million resort community fifty miles west of Las Vegas. The resort features a dozen shooting ranges, a firearms pro shop, and a community armory. The highlight: a combat obstacle course featuring a five-story tower and a twisted maze of tunnels.

3. Barfly Finds "Happy Hour" Depressing

TABLOID Barfly to barmaid: "Sure, Yuppies fill the place from 4 P.M. to 6 P.M. But where are they at 10 A.M. when you need 'em?"

4. Cars Average 190 MPH On Country Road

TRUTH The fastest-traveled highway in the world is ninety miles of asphalt between the tiny towns of Lund and Hiko in White Pine County, Nevada. Twice a year, officials throw the speed limit out the window and allow drivers to travel as quickly as they possibly can. Veteran hot-rodder Chuck Shafer set a public-highway speed record by averaging 198 MPH over the entire route. He hit a top speed of 212 MPH in his souped-up Chrysler LeBaron.

5. Beauty Queen Dethroned For Being Too Thin

TABLOID When it comes to beauty competitions, it's hard to be too thin. But you can be too young. That was the case for Jannette Velazquez, who won the annual Puerto Rican Queen pageant in Vineland, New Jersey. Contestants are required to be at least sixteen, but Jannette was only fifteen when she took the crown. She had lied about her age on the application, but eventually the truth came out. First runner-up, Karen Torres, sixteen, was then awarded the title.

GAME 10

Are the following headlines **TRUTH or TABLOID?**
(See next page for correct answers.)

1. **Football Fan Buried Beneath 50-Yard Line**

2. **City Fire Truck Seeks Sponsors**

3. **Naked Man Showers In Car Wash**

4. **City Says New Cars Must Remain Indoors**

5. **Cops Bug Crucifix To Catch Frisky Priest**

1. FOOTBALL FAN BURIED BENEATH 50-YARD LINE

TABLOID However, when Paul Wellener died unexpectedly, his family wanted to honor his memory with a salute to his lifelong passion for football. So Wellener's widow, Mary Ann, and his son, Paul, bought three pairs of old stadium seats at auction. Three Rivers Stadium, home to the Pittsburgh Steelers, pocketed twenty-one hundred dollars in the deal—and the Wellener family acquired the perfect gravestone for dad.

2. CITY FIRE TRUCK SEEKS SPONSORS

TRUTH The tiny community of Stockertown, Pennsylvania—population 650—needed a fire truck, so they bought one. Suddenly strapped for cash, the town couldn't make the payments. Not to worry. The city council president and the fire chief came up with a solution: selling advertising space on the new truck. How's that for ingenuity?

3. NAKED MAN SHOWERS IN CAR WASH

TABLOID No one has done this yet, but a naked driver in Waterloo, Ontario, crashed into six cars after weaving in and out of traffic. He left the scene dressed in handcuffs.

4. CITY SAYS NEW CARS MUST REMAIN INDOORS

TRUTH Trying to maintain its aura of suburban orderliness, Wilsonville, Oregon, banned new-car dealers from displaying vehicles outdoors. As a result, all cars remain inside cavernous showrooms until they're driven home by purchasers.

5. COPS BUG CRUCIFIX TO CATCH FRISKY PRIEST

TABLOID But here's one about a bad guy who, in a sense, "bugged" himself: When a police officer in Carlisle, Pennsylvania, phoned suspect Randy Smeltz about a stolen radio, someone answered without saying anything, then put down the receiver. The officer eavesdropped as Smeltz discussed his marijuana-growing operation with a visitor. A police cruiser was dispatched to the scene, where Smeltz was arrested for manufacturing and selling marijuana.

CHAPTER 4

THE WORLD

Take the bizarre behavior of one local weirdo, multiply that by a billion or so, and you've got the approximate number of oddballs that inhabit this great globe of ours. This chapter is dedicated to their envelope-stretching activities, as reported in the world section of newspapers, magazines, and other media outlets. As you'll see, from the South Pole to Cuba with a nostalgic step back to ancient Mayan civilization, there's no limit to what human beings will do.

GAME 1

Are the following headlines **TRUTH *or* TABLOID?**
(See next page for correct answers.)

1. **SPOON-STEALERS PLAGUE NOBEL PRIZE AWARDS DINNER**

2. **NOBEL WINNERS MUST ACCEPT PRIZE IN SWEDISH**

3. **POLITICALLY CORRECT CANADIAN SCHOOL BANS REFERENCES TO URANUS**

4. **ILLEGAL ALIEN FOUND DISGUISED AS CAR SEAT**

5. **THE ENGLISH GENTLEMAN SHOULDN'T LOOK TOO SMART**

1. Spoon-Stealers Plague Nobel Prize Awards Dinner

TRUTH In 1991, $1.6 million in new table settings were designed for the lavish Nobel dinner, in part because more than one hundred coffee spoons had been stolen in prior years by souvenir-hunting geniuses. Another Nobel fact: Each year, the menu is kept a state secret until the 1,373 guests arrive. Yet, even with all the fuss, sometimes an entrée sounds less than spectacular, like one at the 1999 dinner described as "lamb wrapped in cabbage."

2. Nobel Winners Must Accept Prize In Swedish

TABLOID Actually, each Nobel honoree is allowed to speak his or her own language at the ceremonies in Stockholm. A major event in Sweden, the awards show is broadcast live on TV, no doubt keeping millions on the edge of their sensible IKEA teakwood sofas.

3. Politically Correct Canadian School Bans References To Uranus

TABLOID As a matter of fact, the nine-year-old in me couldn't resist mentioning the planet that has entertained elementary school science classes since the big bang.

4. Illegal Alien Found Disguised As Car Seat

TRUTH Enrique Canchola, forty-two, of Mexico, was found by United States customs officials in the backseat of a van—make that *as* the backseat of a van—attempting to enter the country illegally. Friends somehow slipped Enrique upright beneath the upholstery, then wrapped duct tape around his arms and head, in an effort to make him look like part of the interior.

5. The English Gentleman Shouldn't Look Too Smart

TRUTH According to *The Butler Book*, the English gentleman likes his clothes to look well worn and lived in, quite the opposite of "smart," in this gentleman's opinion.

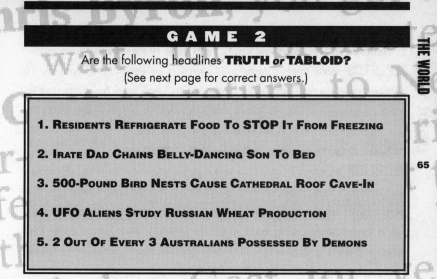

GAME 2

Are the following headlines **TRUTH or TABLOID?**

(See next page for correct answers.)

1. RESIDENTS REFRIGERATE FOOD TO STOP IT FROM FREEZING

2. IRATE DAD CHAINS BELLY-DANCING SON TO BED

3. 500-POUND BIRD NESTS CAUSE CATHEDRAL ROOF CAVE-IN

4. UFO ALIENS STUDY RUSSIAN WHEAT PRODUCTION

5. 2 OUT OF EVERY 3 AUSTRALIANS POSSESSED BY DEMONS

1. RESIDENTS REFRIGERATE FOOD TO STOP IT FROM FREEZING

TRUTH With temperatures in Antarctica plummeting as low as 70 degrees below zero, resident scientists there keep food from freezing by using refrigerators. The insulation that keeps warm temperatures at bay in mild climates has the opposite effect at the South Pole.

2. IRATE DAD CHAINS BELLY-DANCING SON TO BED

TRUTH Mahmut Dagyolu, a teenage belly dancer in Istanbul, Turkey, was chained to his bed for three days to prevent him from performing at local nightclubs. A word in the dancing boy's defense: Male belly dancing has a long history dating back to Ottoman times. Men would cover their faces with veils and entertain their brethren because women were barred from performing. But for the sake of Istanbul clubbers, let's hope that Mahmut's provocative belly isn't matted with thick, wiry body hair.

3. 500-POUND BIRD NESTS CAUSE CATHEDRAL ROOF CAVE-IN

TRUTH Storks caused the roof of a sixteenth-century cathedral in Alaraz, Spain, to cave in. Twenty-three of the giant birds each built quarter-ton nests atop the roof, resulting in dangerous sagging, said Marceliano Iglesias, mayor of the small town.

4. UFO ALIENS STUDY RUSSIAN WHEAT PRODUCTION

TRUTH The reputable (at least it used to be) Itar-Tass news agency reported that Russian officials have discovered new crop circles in a wheat field outside Maikop in the Krasnodar region. Similar circles were found there several years ago as well. According to Tass, "Officials of the region's Emergency Situations Department say this suggests that the beings had come back for more soil samples."

5. 2 OUT OF EVERY 3 AUSTRALIANS POSSESSED BY DEMONS

TABLOID Although many Australians are often possessed by spirits of some sort, it's usually in the guise of a can of Foster's or 4X, which some teetotalers see as the work of the devil himself.

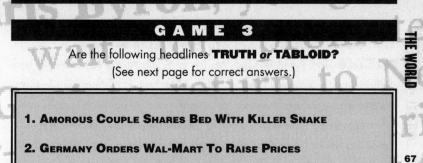

GAME 3

Are the following headlines **TRUTH or TABLOID?**
(See next page for correct answers.)

1. Amorous Couple Shares Bed With Killer Snake

2. Germany Orders Wal-Mart To Raise Prices

3. Trinidad Issues Britney Spears Postage Stamp

4. Far Out! Tanzania Issues Jerry Garcia Stamp

5. Ancient Mayans Lived In Suburbs, Shopped At Malls

1. AMOROUS COUPLE SHARES BED WITH KILLER SNAKE

TRUTH Bruce and Margie Warren of South Africa unknowingly bedded down with a deadly black mamba. After the two of them heard noises, a snake expert located the seven-and-a-half-foot mamba in the headboard of the couple's bed. Rumor has it that in the subsequent divorce, Bruce gained custody of the snake and the headboard, while Margie, having hit it off well with him during their initial encounter, retained the snake expert.

2. GERMANY ORDERS WAL-MART TO RAISE PRICES

TRUTH Government officials accused Wal-Mart of being too competitive and ordered the giant retailer to raise prices on milk, flour, cooking oil, and other household staples.

3. TRINIDAD ISSUES BRITNEY SPEARS POSTAGE STAMP

TABLOID Even though the nation has issued many such novelties, it has yet to make Britney's belly button lickable by anyone who purchases a stamp.

4. FAR OUT! TANZANIA ISSUES JERRY GARCIA STAMP

TRUTH In an act of near-mythical significance to certain Greatful Dead fans, the African nation issued a stamp featuring the bearded, beatific guitarist.

5. ANCIENT MAYANS LIVED IN SUBURBS, SHOPPED AT MALLS

TRUTH The ancient Mayans of Central America had their own form of suburban sprawl. University of Central Florida archaeologists at the Caracol in Belize recently uncovered evidence of suburbs and shopping malls surrounding an urban core.

Mayan daughter: "Mom, I'm going to the mall to walk around with the other virgins."

Mayan mom: "Okay, just don't get yourself thrown into a volcano."

GAME 4

Are the following headlines **TRUTH or TABLOID?**
(See next page for correct answers.)

1. **NEW MISS SOMALIA WINS ETHIOPIAN DREAM VACATION**

2. **NOSE-JOB BANDAGES ALL THE RAGE IN IRAN**

3. **RANDY PEACOCKS OF THE RICH TERRORIZE BRITISH VILLAGES**

4. **THIS JUST IN! BIG BOOBS ARE BACK IN BRAZIL**

5. **SOUTH AFRICAN STUDENTS TURN IN THEIR AXES**

And now, for the CORRECT ANSWERS to GAME 4:

1. NEW MISS SOMALIA WINS ETHIOPIAN DREAM VACATION

TABLOID Perhaps it was a round-trip ticket to glorious Angola.

2. NOSE-JOB BANDAGES ALL THE RAGE IN IRAN

TRUTH It has become a badge of honor for upscale Iranian women to wear their post–nose-surgery bandages in public. "It's just like women's clothing," says Tehran plastic surgeon Dr. Ali Akbar Jalali. "Things go in and out of fashion."

3. RANDY PEACOCKS OF THE RICH TERRORIZE BRITISH VILLAGES

TRUTH In a scene out of a fifties Hammer horror movie, flocks of peacocks are attacking innocent children and destroying beloved gardens in several picturesque English villages in the countryside north of London. Officials believe that marauding male birds have fled the sprawling estates of the upper crust in search of peahens to mate with. The villagers are simply in the way.

Christopher Lee: "Good lord, what sort of diabolical beasts have you created?"

Peter Cushing: "Randy, class-conscious peacocks!"

4. THIS JUST IN! BIG BOOBS ARE BACK IN BRAZIL

TRUTH Breaking news! In Chapter 1, Game 3, headline 2, I revealed to you that for decades, breast reductions were the most popular form of cosmetic surgery in Brazil. But since that headline was written, women have done a complete about-face . . . or whatever. Almost overnight, breast enlargements have become the rage. In fact, according to *The Wall Street Journal,* there's a shortage of implants! Why? A series of TV celebrities, like the winner of the Brazilian version of *Survivor,* gave implants a bounce by raving publicly about the benefits. There's even a year-long wait at some clinics. Now, back to our regular report . . .

5. SOUTH AFRICAN STUDENTS TURN IN THEIR AXES

TRUTH About one thousand schoolchildren threw their axes and knives into a Johannesburg river as part of a ceremony to help eradicate crime in South African schools.

GAME 5

Are the following headlines **TRUTH** *or* **TABLOID?**
(See next page for correct answers.)

1. TRANSPARENT PISSOIR LOWERS VICE RATE

2. MEXICO EDGES CANADA TO WIN STUPIDITY TITLE

3. FINLAND INTRODUCES THE $44,000 TRAFFIC TICKET

4. OPTIMISTIC EXPLORER DRAGGED BOATS THROUGH THE OUTBACK

5. "MILITARY GRADE" ODOR DISABLES COLOMBIAN MOB

1. TRANSPARENT PISSOIR LOWERS VICE RATE

TABLOID Public urinals haven't gone in that direction yet, but two Australian artists have created "Pissoir," a prefabricated wall unit that can be installed in an existing gallery toilet. They say, "The urinal is sensitized to allow participants (both male and female) to draw using their urine. The resultant drawings are displayed real-time in the gallery space, then automatically uploaded onto the Internet."

2. MEXICO EDGES CANADA TO WIN STUPIDITY TITLE

TABLOID U.S.A.! U.S.A.! U.S.A.! That's right—not Mexico but the United States barely beat Canada in a stupidity contest. While 60 percent of Canadians failed a ten-question quiz on Canadian facts and history, slightly more than 60 percent of Americans failed a similar test about the United States, giving us a well-deserved win. Go team.

3. FINLAND INTRODUCES THE $44,000 TRAFFIC TICKET

TRUTH If you're visiting Finland, bad driving will cost you—especially if you're rich. The higher your income, the higher the fine. In one case, Finnish hockey star Temmu Selanne was fined forty-four thousand dollars for reckless driving.

4. OPTIMISTIC EXPLORER DRAGGED BOATS THROUGH THE OUTBACK

TRUTH Thomas Mitchell was a pioneering explorer of Australia's outback, confident that he'd find a river or a lake. So he and his party dragged two wooden boats behind them for three thousand miles. The boats never touched water.

5. "MILITARY GRADE" ODOR DISABLES COLOMBIAN MOB

TABLOID No army is at work behind the scenes, designing a way to render protestors helpless with stink. But the United States military is into sound in a big way. Long under development has been a device with a bass rumble so low that it causes anyone within earshot to lose control of their bowels. There is still one insurmountable hurdle: preventing American troops from taking the same hit.

GAME 6

Are the following headlines **TRUTH** *or* **TABLOID**?
(See next page for correct answers.)

1. **RUSSIAN FIRM INTRODUCES RENT-TO-OWN SPOUSE**

2. **RUSSIA RAISES FUNDS WITH XXX-RATED STAMPS**

3. **CHOCOLATE-COVERED PORK FAT = RUSSIAN CANDY BAR**

4. **STRIPPERS WOO RUSSIAN VOTERS**

5. **POLICE IGNORE MOSCOW MAN TRAPPED INSIDE GARBAGE TRUCK**

1. RUSSIAN FIRM INTRODUCES RENT-TO-OWN SPOUSE

TABLOID Regardless, Lenin probably never foresaw that the former Soviets would become one of the world's leading producers of mail-order brides.

2. RUSSIA RAISES FUNDS WITH XXX-RATED STAMPS

TABLOID Since it collapsed, the former Soviet Union has sold off everything, from pigeon-stained statues of Lenin to hammer-and-sickle memorabilia, but no stamps with Stalin in a compromising position just yet.

3. CHOCOLATE-COVERED PORK FAT = RUSSIAN CANDY BAR

TRUTH Just imagine the condition of your arteries after a couple of these. But this is a commercially manufactured candy bar most popular in eastern Russia, where recent figures show that the average lifespan is falling.

4. STRIPPERS WOO RUSSIAN VOTERS

TABLOID In warmer climes, though, they appear to go for that sort of thing. In an attempt to woo women, male exotic dancers stripped for the candidate of their choice at an election rally in Mexico City. About 150,000 people attended the huge outdoor function.

5. POLICE IGNORE MOSCOW MAN TRAPPED INSIDE GARBAGE TRUCK

TRUTH This is a cautionary tale about vodka and the indifference of Moscow police. On January, 9, 2002, after a hard night on the town, twenty-five-year-old Taras Shugayev awoke from a stupor to find himself trapped in the back end of a moving garbage truck. Inches from huge blades that were slowly mulching the refuse, Taras frantically dialed the police on his cell phone. Unfortunately, rather than send a cop to the scene, bored police dispatchers advised poor Taras to bang on a wall to alert the truck's driver. According to a transcript of the call, Taras's last words were, "This is it. I think I am suffocating. This is it." The next day, he was reported missing by his family, and a search for his remains was launched in a likely landfill.

GAME 7

Are the following headlines **TRUTH** *or* **TABLOID?**
(See next page for correct answers.)

1. RICE IS FOR WEAKLINGS, SAY RED CHINESE

2. CHINA PLANS TO CONQUER U.S. WITH MILK

3. 12-FINGERED PIANIST BANNED FROM CHINESE COMPETITION

4. CICADA TRAINER NAMED CHINA'S "FASTEST-RISING"
   ENTERTAINER

5. CHINESE ACTIVISTS PLAN TO BAN SUSHI

75

1. Rice Is For Weaklings, Say Red Chinese

TRUTH Susan Glosser, professor of Chinese history at Lewis and Clark College in Oregon, says that rice and vegetables are sometimes termed "weakling foods" in China, which fits into the late, lamented Chairman Mao's long-term plan for world domination. Or, as Mao said in his famous *Red Book*, "To defeat wicked foreigners, open restaurants in their homelands. Make them weak with rice, then strike final blow with MSG and very high-fat sauces!"

2. China Plans To Conquer U.S. With Milk

TABLOID But here's another fascinating tidbit from Professor Susan Glosser of Lewis and Clark College: Some mainland Chinese feel they can ingest the power of a culture by eating its food.

3. 12-Fingered Pianist Banned From Chinese Competition

TABLOID According to a staff of highly trained researchers, there are no living twelve-fingered Chinese pianists. My cousin Vern had eleven fingers, but he couldn't play the dial on a radio.

4. Cicada Trainer Named China's "Fastest-Rising" Entertainer

TABLOID While it is undeniable that *qigong* master Sun Min Xin has a very special talent, his ability to train cicadas has yet to lead to major media success. Thus far, his fame appears limited to a captioned photo in *The Four Major Mysteries of Mainland China*, a book about "recurring paranormal phenomena" behind the "Bamboo Curtain." The photo shows Sun Min Xin with his bare arm against a tree. The caption, written by the book's author, Paul Dong, states: "When he places his hand close to the cicadas, the cicadas on the tree crawl down the tree. It has been demonstrated hundreds of times. The photo shows him performing the art."

5. Chinese Activists Plan To Ban Sushi

TABLOID Actually, their target is chopsticks. China goes through forty-five billion pairs of chopsticks every year—that's about twenty-five million trees. Activists across the country hope to replace disposable chopsticks with spoons or reusable plastic chopsticks.

GAME 8

Are the following headlines **TRUTH** *or* **TABLOID**?
(See next page for correct aswers.)

1. OHIO "GARAGE BAND" SCORES VIETNAM CHART-TOPPER

2. MILLIONS HONOR SEVERED, SMOKED HUMAN HEADS

3. "VOODOO POPE" CHOSEN BY SUN

4. CUBA'S SPIES MUST MOONLIGHT TO MAKE ENDS MEET

5. EARTH IS AN ALIEN LANDFILL, CLAIMS ARCHAEOLOGIST

1. OHIO "GARAGE BAND" SCORES VIETNAM CHART-TOPPER

TABLOID Sadly, at the time this was written, the Socialist Republic of Vietnam did not have a pop chart.

2. MILLIONS HONOR SEVERED, SMOKED HUMAN HEADS

TRUTH Nearly two million ethnic Dayaks live in Borneo, the world's third-largest island. Until a hundred years ago, head-hunting was an essential part of the Dayak religion, with the heads preserved by wood-smoking. Recently, the Dayaks returned to their head-hunting ways, decapitating thousands of their non-Dayak neighbors. According to Bahing Djimat, secretary of the Dayak Community Organization, "We have been patient for a long time and can't take it anymore."

3. "VOODOO POPE" CHOSEN BY SUN

TRUTH Voodoo is the state religion in Benin, a West African nation of 6.3 million people. Awhile back, Sosa Guedehoungue, the nation's so-called voodoo pope, died at the age of eighty-nine. A new leader was chosen when the right ray of sunlight shone on the right man at the right time. Travel tip: Stay out of the sun in Benin, unless you want to become the spiritual leader of millions.

4. CUBA'S SPIES MUST MOONLIGHT TO MAKE ENDS MEET

TRUTH Castro pays his United States–based spies so little money that they often need to work two jobs to make ends meet, leaving them precious little time to spy. For example, an agent named Mario worked nine hours a day at a Miami food-seasoning factory, then spent another seven and a half hours as a maintenance man at the home arena of the Miami Heat. The details came to light during a Florida spy trial.

5. EARTH IS AN ALIEN LANDFILL, CLAIMS ARCHAEOLOGIST

TABLOID That doesn't mean that we're not leaving lots of earthly garbage in outer space. According to *Discovering Archaeology* magazine, our orbiting space garbage includes bolts, springs, clamps, and almost two hundred actual garbage bags—contents unknown—released from the former Mir space station.

GAME 9

Are the following headlines **TRUTH** *or* **TABLOID**?
(See next page for correct answers.)

1. **ELEPHANTS CRIPPLE INDIA'S AIR FORCE**

2. **ACTIVIST SAYS QUAKE DROVE COWS INSANE**

3. **WORMS COMMUNICATE WITH INDIAN RESEARCHER**

4. **INDIA: ONE PERSON AN HOUR DIES FROM FRIGHT**

5. **HERSHEY'S KISSES BANNED AS "EROTIC"**

1. ELEPHANTS CRIPPLE INDIA'S AIR FORCE

TRUTH In a nightmare scenario, herds of wild elephants attacked for several evenings straight, terrifying pilots and ground staff at the Tezpur military airfield in northeast India. Strategic night sorties of the Indian Air Force were crippled. More than 150 raging pachyderms participated in the raids.

2. ACTIVIST SAYS QUAKE DROVE COWS INSANE

TRUTH A massive earthquake in India caused cows to exhibit bizarre behavior, according to Kalpana Patel of the Vadodara Society for Prevention of Cruelty to Animals. For more than a month, three thousand cows at the SPCA shelter began to walk in circles. "They're not going anywhere," Patel said at the time. "They're just in a constant rotary movement." There were no reports of Prozac having been administered.

3. WORMS COMMUNICATE WITH INDIAN RESEARCHER

TABLOID If a worm could talk, what would it say? 1. "I love squirming on the sidewalk in the rain." 2. "Yes, I *do* have a head." 3. "Ick to you, too!"

4. INDIA: ONE PERSON AN HOUR DIES FROM FRIGHT

TABLOID Actually, nearly one person an hour—more than eighty-five hundred a year—die from the bite of the king cobra. Despite this, the frightening, extremely dangerous snake is also an object of worship to many rural Indians. It is honored at festivals and appears on floats during parades. If a king cobra enters a home, nothing is done to harm the snake, even after it has bitten a family member. During festivals, celebrants routinely turn up at hospitals in the Indian countryside seeking treatment for snakebite.

5. HERSHEY'S KISSES BANNED AS "EROTIC"

TABLOID Candy is okay, but actual kissing has long been banned in Indian movies and on Indian TV, even though some hip Bombay advertising creatives are battling to have the prohibition overturned.

GAME 10

Are the following headlines **TRUTH** *or* **TABLOID?**
(See next page for correct answers.)

1. L.A. Gang-Banger Nominated For Nobel Peace Prize

2. Wacky Aussie Wants Sex Positions As Olympic Sport

3. Brit Groupie Offers Guide To "60-Second Sex"

4. Icy Glacier Towers Above Steamy Tropical Isle

5. Meal Is Free If It Ain't Alive When You Eat It

1. L.A. GANG-BANGER NOMINATED FOR NOBEL PEACE PRIZE

TRUTH When Stanley Williams cofounded the infamous "Crips" street gang in 1971, he had no idea he'd one day be nominated for the 2001 Nobel Peace Prize. Williams, a.k.a. "Big Took," was found guilty of murdering four rival-gang members in 1981. He's now on death row in San Quentin. But during his time behind bars he created the Internet Project for Street Peace, which allows at-risk youths to communicate via E-mail. The effort gained the notice of Swiss Parliament member Mario Fehr, who nominated Williams for the prestigious award.

2. WACKY AUSSIE WANTS SEX POSITIONS AS OLYMPIC SPORT

TABLOID Wacky Australian to Olympic committee: "The event could be divided into two parts, compulsory and freestyle. In the compulsory section, athletes would be judged on the skill with which they assume the required positions. The freestyle portion would be set to music and put the spotlight on the participants' creativity as they grapple on the mat."

3. BRIT GROUPIE OFFERS GUIDE TO "60-SECOND SEX"

TABLOID You should know, however, that in the minute it takes you to play Game 10, a pop star somewhere will have had sex, from foreplay to signing the requisite autograph.

4. ICY GLACIER TOWERS ABOVE STEAMY TROPICAL ISLE

TRUTH Adventurous snowboarders take note: The Ice Age–born Meren Glacier sits atop the Carstensz Mountains in the equatorial South Seas nation of Irian Jaya.

5. MEAL IS FREE IF IT AIN'T ALIVE WHEN YOU EAT IT

TRUTH Warning: Squeamish people should skip what follows. A restaurant in Hoi An, Vietnam, serves a dish called Gaping Fish. Their recipe: Take one large fish of any type. Insert an eight-inch bamboo stick through its mouth, piercing the brain in order to paralyze the fish. Do not gut. Dip fish vertically into hot oil, making sure that the head does not go under. DO NOT LET FISH DIE. Remove from oil, and remove bamboo sticks. If fish opens its mouth, or "gapes," it is still alive. Serve to customer. If fish dies before customer cuts into the cooked flesh, it is free. You were warned.

CHAPTER 5

GOSSIP

PAGE

Gossip is good, to paraphrase a noted felon. It's mainstream entertainment, whether the subject is celebrities, next-door neighbors, or the unsuspecting cuckold who just left the party. The exchange of gossip may even be the glue that holds our complex human society together, bonding us in the same way that mutual lice-picking does for an extended family of chimpanzees. Perhaps the very best aspect of gossip, though, is that it's loads of fun even when it's not true.

GAME 1

Are the following headlines **TRUTH** *or* **TABLOID?**
(See next page for correct answers.)

1. **CHER TO PLAY SONNY IN BIZARRE BIOPIC**

2. **"I'M BALDING AND PAUNCHY," ADMITS FLOCK OF SEAGULLS LEAD SINGER**

3. **BILLIONAIRE TAKES $9 MILLION VACATION**

4. **MUSCLE-BOUND BILLIONAIRE PUMPS IRON WITH GOLD DUMBBELLS**

5. **SPURNED BY ONE TWIN, HE MARRIES THE OTHER!**

And now, for the CORRECT ANSWERS to GAME 1:

1. CHER TO PLAY SONNY IN BIZARRE BIOPIC

TABLOID Rumor has it, though, that Johnny Depp has undergone extensive wig fittings.

2. "I'M BALDING AND PAUNCHY," ADMITS FLOCK OF SEAGULLS LEAD SINGER

TRUTH Infamous during the eighties for his weirdly combed hair, fiftyish Mike Score confessed on the group's website that he doesn't have much left. What has he been doing for the last twenty years? "I've been getting old and fat," he admitted.

3. BILLIONAIRE TAKES $9 MILLION VACATION

TRUTH Microsoft cofounder Paul Allen once rented a luxury cruise ship, the *Radisson Seven Seas Navigator,* for a late-summer vacation. He invited such guests as Paul McCartney and Dan Aykroyd to join him for four days of fun and frolic in St. Petersburg, Russia. Highlights included helicopter rides, sumptuous meals, tall-ship cruises, and the opportunity to fire weapons, including the AK-47 "and a variety of other handguns formerly used by the KGB." Total cost estimated in excess of nine million dollars.

4. MUSCLE-BOUND BILLIONAIRE PUMPS IRON WITH GOLD DUMBBELLS

TABLOID Still, not a bad idea. Gold is about four times heavier than iron, and it's a pretty color.

5. SPURNED BY ONE TWIN, HE MARRIES THE OTHER!

TRUTH At twenty-one, shy Lauren Daniels met twins Sharon and Selah Arends, sixteen, upon returning to Paso Robles, California, at the end of World War II. He found the nerve to ask Selah for a date, but Selah showed up at the baseball game with another guy. Apparently not one to be spurned, Lauren set his cap for Sharon instead. After a three-year courtship, they married in 1950.

GAME 2

Are the following headlines **TRUTH** *or* **TABLOID?**
(See next page for correct answers.)

1. JIM CARREY POSSESSED BY DECEASED SPIRIT!

2. HUGH HEFNER FAKES LOW IQ TO MEET GIRLS

3. JEFFREY DAHMER WAS A VEGETARIAN, EXCEPT FOR PEOPLE

4. TITANIC: KATE WINSLET'S LEFT BREAST WAS A STAND-IN

5. "I'M NOT REALLY COOL," SAYS BRUTALLY HONEST DAVID
   SPADE

1. JIM CARREY POSSESSED BY DECEASED SPIRIT!

TRUTH Breathless press reports claimed that numerous people on the set of *Man on the Moon* said that Jim Carrey was "not there" during filming, and that he was completely possessed by the spirit of Andy Kaufman, the late comedian he portrayed. The real Jim was present only once or twice, according to another observer. When the movie bombed, the publicity department banished the ghost of Mr. Kaufman to that special part of hell reserved by Hollywood for the unpopular dead, never to haunt Jim Carrey again.

2. HUGH HEFNER FAKES LOW IQ TO MEET GIRLS

TABLOID Hugh can get any woman he wants, unlike Thomas Madison of Aloha, Oregon, who advertised in the newspaper that he was mentally disabled and incontinent and needed a caregiver to come to his home. Madison did all this, allegedly, as a way to meet women. Fortunately, the first woman he hired called the police. Mr. Lonelyhearts went to jail, charged with attempting to compel prostitution. Bail was set at two hundred thousand dollars.

3. JEFFREY DAHMER WAS A VEGETARIAN, EXCEPT FOR PEOPLE

TABLOID Vegetarians rejoice! The Milwaukee cannibal ate a variety of meats. An employee of a chocolate factory, Dahmer's cherished dream, according to rumor, was to one day work for the one owned by Willie Wonka.

4. TITANIC: KATE WINSLET'S LEFT BREAST WAS A STAND-IN

TABLOID Both were hers, as Kate has revealed in many movies since.

5. "I'M NOT REALLY COOL," SAYS BRUTALLY HONEST DAVID SPADE

TRUTH Hollywood has brutalized film fans with way too many David Spade movies, as even the immortal Joe Dirt seems to know. As Spade revealed in a Mr. Showbiz.com bio, "Basically, I'm not really cool, it's more of an optical illusion. But if it works, I'll take it." Film fans of conscience: We stopped Paulie Shore! We *can* stop David Spade!

GAME 3

Are the following headlines **TRUTH** *or* **TABLOID?**
(See next page for correct answers.)

1. "HIRE ME, NFL," SAYS CONDOLEEZA RICE

2. RABBI HELPS MICHAEL JACKSON FIND KOSHER SEX

3. FAMED RACE DRIVER FEARS RUSH HOUR MORE

4. WESLEY SNIPES FEARS NOTHING!

5. COLD PIZZA MADE OZZY OSBOURNE QUIT DRINKING

1. "HIRE ME, NFL," SAYS CONDOLEEZA RICE

TRUTH The brainy, articulate National Security Adviser to President Bush once told a women's magazine that her "dream job is to be NFL commissioner. I love football, especially the Cleveland Browns." Her number-two passion is shopping (for cruise missiles and shoulder pads?).

2. RABBI HELPS MICHAEL JACKSON FIND KOSHER SEX

TRUTH Apparently, Rabbi Shmuley Boteach, author of *Kosher Sex*, has found his mission—acting as matchmaker for singer Michael Jackson. The two have become fast friends, and Michael gratefully announced that "Rabbi Shmuley keeps telling me he's going to find me the perfect woman." Wasn't that Lisa Presley?

3. FAMED RACE DRIVER FEARS RUSH HOUR MORE

TABLOID Winston Cup winner Jeff Gordon told Larry King, "To be honest, I have no real interest in automobiles. I can drive anything. I don't really care. I love racing around the track, but away from my work, I much prefer boating or flying."

4. WESLEY SNIPES FEARS NOTHING!

TRUTH Throughout the actor's brilliant career, he's had the opportunity to play many fearless men. But Wesley also says that in real life, he fears nothing. In fact, the superstar told a reporter, "I'm most afraid of being afraid of anything." Whatever that means.

5. COLD PIZZA MADE OZZY OSBOURNE QUIT DRINKING

TRUTH The former Black Sabbath lead singer says he gave up the bottle because he got tired of waking up with a cold pizza stuck to his face. (Reminds me of the audience after twelve hours at Ozzfest.)

GAME 4

Are the following headlines **TRUTH** *or* **TABLOID**?
(See next page for correct answers.)

1. OFFICE GOSSIP IS GOOD FOR BUSINESS

2. BRAZILIAN CITY BANS GOSSIP

3. TO FOIL OFFICE GOSSIPS, USE CIA TACTICS

4. GOSSIPS ARE A STEP UP THE EVOLUTIONARY LADDER

5. FIGHT GOSSIP WITH GOSSIP, SAYS EXPERT

1. Office Gossip Is Good For Business

TRUTH "Gossip is the cement which holds organisations together," Judith Doyle of the Industrial Society told the BBC. She even suggests that businesses provide a coffee area or lunch room where employees can engage in constructive gossip. Her number-one tip: Bring back the tea trolley that was once a fixture in the British workplace.

2. Brazilian City Bans Gossip

TRUTH In Cascavel, Brazil, city employees are banned from gossiping during work hours. Anyone caught doing so is fired.

3. To Foil Office Gossips, Use CIA Tactics

TABLOID Implementing a disinformation campaign about who stole your last doughnut will not stop the sluts, pimps, drunks, and nut-jobs in your department from spreading malicious gossip about you.

4. Gossips Are A Step Up The Evolutionary Ladder

TRUTH Author Robin Dunbar contends in *Grooming, Gossip, and the Evolution of Language* that humans gossip because we don't groom each other. Picking fleas off a neighbor's back helps a small community of apes bond with one another, but our advanced, more complex society doesn't allow for such intimacy, so we gossip about celebrities, family members, and friends in order to feel as close as apes do during a loving tick-removal session. In other words, professional gossip columnists like Liz Smith are the "designated flea pickers" of sophisticated human society.

5. Fight Gossip With Gossip, Says Expert

TABLOID Actually, an expert from *Workforce* magazine says that among the best ways for a business to combat office gossip are to keep employees informed and to deal with rumors immediately. He offers no advice on how to find who stole your doughnut.

GAME 5

Are the following headlines **TRUTH** *or* **TABLOID**?
(See next page for correct answers.)

1. **THE WHITE HOUSE IS INFESTED WITH RATS**

2. **GEORGE WASHINGTON SMELLS LIKE WET SHEEP, GOSSIPS SAY**

3. **KING LOUIS XII KISSES EVERY WOMAN IN NORMANDY!**

4. **KING LOUIS XIII INVENTS THE "FRENCH KISS"**

5. **BRITISH P.M. DOESN'T SPEAK FOR 8 YEARS**

1. THE WHITE HOUSE IS INFESTED WITH RATS

TRUTH Due to its age and urban location, the White House has a long-standing rat problem. Huge, ugly rats have been spotted in the White House living area—and even in the outdoor swimming pool.

2. GEORGE WASHINGTON SMELLS LIKE WET SHEEP, GOSSIPS SAY

TABLOID However, John Adams, the second president of the United States, did make a connection between Washington and the animals that produced woolen wigs. Adams referred to Washington as "Old Mutton-head," a more or less affectionate term of the times.

3. KING LOUIS XII KISSES EVERY WOMAN IN NORMANDY!

TRUTH King Louis XII was a merry old soul, a merry old soul was he, and under the guise of granting his royal benediction, he convinced every woman in Normandy to plant one on him!

4. KING LOUIS XIII INVENTS THE "FRENCH KISS"

TABLOID Actually, the earliest known depiction of the deep kiss dates back to around 200 B.C. Archaeologists discovered it on erotic Mochica pottery in—Peru.

5. BRITISH P.M. DOESN'T SPEAK FOR 8 YEARS

TABLOID It's interesting to note, though, that a member of the House of Lords didn't speak for twenty-one years. According to reliable reports, the twelfth Earl of Waldegrave took his seat in the House of Lords in 1936—and wasn't moved to say anything until 1957. According to much less reliable reports, due to a large truck passing by, no one heard him.

GAME 6

Are the following headlines **TRUTH** *or* **TABLOID?**
(See next page for correct answers.)

1. **HARRISON FORD GOT PAID TO LAY PIPE**

2. **JOE PESCI SEES WITH ANOTHER MAN'S EYES!**

3. **DARYL HANNAH: SUICIDAL MEN TURN HER ON**

4. **KATE WINSLET IS TIRED OF SEX**

5. **RICHARD GERE ADMITS HE PUTS OUT GARBAGE**

1. HARRISON FORD GOT PAID TO LAY PIPE

TRUTH After failing to break into the big time in the early 1970s, Ford earned his living in the construction business. The big shots finally noticed him in 1973, when he played a cool street racer in *American Graffiti*. And that was the last time Harrison got paid to saw, hammer, or figure out which was the female end of the pipe.

2. JOE PESCI SEES WITH ANOTHER MAN'S EYES!

TABLOID The tiny actor who played a tough guy in *Goodfellas* and other Martin Scorcese films still relies on his own eyes. But each is a different color, according to reliable industry sources.

3. DARYL HANNAH: SUICIDAL MEN TURN HER ON

TRUTH Daryl earned some gossip-page ink when she described her kind of man: "Oh, you're a drug addict? And down on your luck . . . and depressed and suicidal? I love you." She's just kidding. Or is she????

4. KATE WINSLET IS TIRED OF SEX

TRUTH The gorgeous and talented young actress with a penchant for hot love scenes says doing them is tough and tiring work. Kate told a reporter, "I defy any actor to say it's easy, because it's not." She says it took all day to film a sex scene for *Quills*, which left her "very exhausted."

5. RICHARD GERE ADMITS HE PUTS OUT GARBAGE

TRUTH In a revealing interview with *Biography* magazine, Gere admitted, "I have a very simple life. When you have a home, and a household, and a kid, you're just the guy who takes out the garbage." He did not mention *Intersection*, *Mr. Jones*, or *The Mothman Prophecies*.

GAME 7

Are the following headlines **TRUTH** *or* **TABLOID?**

(See next page for correct answers.)

1. **PRETENDERS SINGER WON'T #&^% MEAT-EATING MEN**

2. **WINONA RYDER ONLY #&^% GUYS WHOSE NAMES START WITH D**

3. **SENATOR ORRIN HATCH SPOTTED IN MOSH PIT**

4. **WORRIED LIZ TAYLOR CAN RECALL ONLY 5 OF 7 HUSBANDS**

5. **DON'T LOOK WHEN KEVIN BACON BUYS PREPARATION H**

1. Pretenders Singer Won't #&^% Meat-Eating Men

TRUTH Chrissie Hynde, an ultrastrict vegetarian, apparently won't have *any* kind of sex with a bloody meat eater, she reported to a meeting of the People for the Ethical Treatment of Animals in Los Angeles. No comment on sleeping with a guy who ate steamed cabbage for dinner.

2. Winona Ryder Only #&^% Guys Whose Names Start With D

TABLOID At least, it seemed that way for a while. A string of five boyfriends included Matt Damon, Johnny Depp, Daniel Day-Lewis, David Duchovny, and a dude named Dave Pirner, from the early nineties rock group Soul Asylum. But then she dated Chris Noth of *Sex in the City* and blew the "D Theory" to hell.

3. Senator Orrin Hatch Spotted In Mosh Pit

TRUTH I doubt that the distinguished gentleman from Utah arrived there by stage-diving, but Bono of U2 spotted him in the mosh pit at one of the rock group's concerts. Said Bono to *O, The Oprah Magazine*: "Just the sight of Orrin Hatch in the mosh pit . . . it's exciting."

4. Worried Liz Taylor Can Recall Only 5 Of 7 Husbands

TABLOID I'm sure Elizabeth Taylor can remember every one of her husbands, but I can count them only with the help of *The Film Encyclopedia*. In chronological order, the roll call is hotel owner Nick Hilton, actor Michael Wilding, producer Mike Todd, singer Eddie Fisher, actor Richard Burton (twice), politician John Warner, and handyman Larry Fortensky.

5. Don't Look When Kevin Bacon Buys Preparation H

TRUTH Kevin admits that actors like to be ogled by their adoring public, but they have their limits. He says when it comes to walking into the drugstore to buy a tube of Preparation H, he doesn't want us to see him. Should we pretend he's buying condoms?

GAME 8

Are the following headlines **TRUTH** *or* **TABLOID?**
(See next page for correct answers.)

1. VICAR VETOES COUPLE'S CHOICE OF WEDDING SONGS

2. ACTRESS SPENDS $6,000 ON FACELIFT—AND NOBODY NOTICES!

3. "FREAK DANCING" ELDERLY COUPLE BOOTED FROM BALLROOM

4. ACTRESS GAINS 75 POUNDS FOR MOVIE THAT DOESN'T GET MADE

5. C-SPAN ASKED TO PUT CAMERA IN KEY SENATE WASHROOM

1. VICAR VETOES COUPLE'S CHOICE OF WEDDING SONGS

TRUTH An angry British couple changed their wedding plans after the vicar told them that their choice of songs was too "nationalistic." The vicar turned thumbs down on "Jerusalem" and "I Vow to Thee My Country."

2. ACTRESS SPENDS $6,000 ON FACELIFT—AND NOBODY NOTICES!

TABLOID If an aging starlet gets a facelift and nobody notices, does it really exist?

3. "FREAK DANCING" ELDERLY COUPLE BOOTED FROM BALLROOM

TABLOID But it's funny how fads can pop up at more or less the same time in wildly different parts of the world. According to *In the Shadow of Mr. Kurtz,* a book about Africa, Congolese youth were bumping and grinding in a style similar to freak dancing several years before the craze hit the United States.

4. ACTRESS GAINS 75 POUNDS FOR MOVIE THAT DOESN'T GET MADE

TABLOID Robert DeNiro started the trend when he gained thirty to forty pounds to play aging boxer Jake LaMotta in the 1980 film *Raging Bull*. But it would be interesting to witness someone gain the weight only to have the film canceled. And sue the producer for, say, a lifetime supply of Abdominizers.

5. C-SPAN ASKED TO PUT CAMERA IN KEY SENATE WASHROOM

TABLOID The Senate men's room is where the deals get done, the complimentary *Penthouses* are read, the phlegm-flecked toupees are reglued, and—when Teddy Kennedy heads for a stall after a lunch of four martinis, deep-fried onion rings, and a two-pound porterhouse—every senator still standing bolts for the exit, and the country doesn't need to see that on C-SPAN.

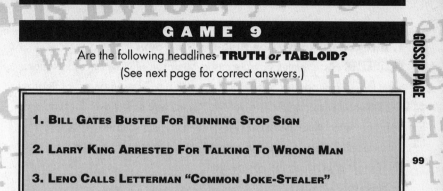

GAME 9

Are the following headlines **TRUTH** *or* **TABLOID?**
(See next page for correct answers.)

1. BILL GATES BUSTED FOR RUNNING STOP SIGN

2. LARRY KING ARRESTED FOR TALKING TO WRONG MAN

3. LENO CALLS LETTERMAN "COMMON JOKE-STEALER"

4. DANNY DEVITO NABBED SNEAKING ONTO DISNEYLAND RIDE

5. RALPH NADER CITED FOR BURNING FALL LEAVES

1. BILL GATES BUSTED FOR RUNNING STOP SIGN

TRUTH His enemies have accused Microsoft of a welter of violations, but it took a courageous Seattle cop to catch Bill Gates in an act of flagrant civil disobedience. In 1977, a youthful Gates was pulled over for running a stop sign, after which he failed to provide a driver's license. The case wasn't pursued, and alleged stop-sign runner Gates went free to pursue the American Dream of crushing the competition.

Steve Jobs: "Drat!"

2. LARRY KING ARRESTED FOR TALKING TO WRONG MAN

TABLOID The legendary CNN talk-show host is able to keep his guests straight, even the ones who appear "live via satellite." By the same token, Larry must have been talking to the wrong kind of people back in 1971 when he was arrested in Miami on charges of grand larceny. King was a talk-radio host at the time, with alleged gambling and other debts.

3. LENO CALLS LETTERMAN "COMMON JOKE-STEALER"

TABLOID The comedians have an intense rivalry, yet neither has accused the other of criminal acts of joke-stealing. Old-school TV comic Milton Berle, on the other hand, was often charged with cribbing jokes from his peers' routines in the 1950s.

Fan to Milton Berle: "Who writes your material?"

Milton Berle to Fan: "Henny Youngman."

4. DANNY DEVITO NABBED SNEAKING ONTO DISNEYLAND RIDE

TABLOID Disney employee: "Can't you see the sign? No children allowed on the Matterhorn under four feet eleven inches tall."

Danny: "But I'm a five-foot-two-inch-tall adult!"

Disney employee: "Tell me one I haven't heard before."

5. RALPH NADER CITED FOR BURNING FALL LEAVES

TABLOID The 2000 Green Party presidential candidate enjoys a modest lifestyle, doesn't own a car, and surely wouldn't rake leaves into a pile and torch them in order to watch the pretty tendrils of smoke pollute the skies of Washington, D.C.

GAME 10

Are the following headlines **TRUTH** *or* **TABLOID?**

(See next page for correct answers.)

1. LIBERACE JOINS RAT PACK IN STEAM ROOM

2. SAMMY'S GLASS EYE BECOMES SINATRA'S KEY RING!

3. CASINO GUARD DOGS PROTECT DEANO FROM JERRY LEWIS

4. JOEY BISHOP: "I EMCEED A LION'S CLUB SMUT SHOW"

5. ACTRESS BREAKS LEG TO MAKE SHIRLEY MacLAINE A STAR

1. LIBERACE JOINS RAT PACK IN STEAM ROOM

TABLOID Although Frank, Sammy, Peter Lawford, Dean Martin, Joey Bishop, and associated swingers often relaxed in Las Vegas steam rooms, there is no record of Liberace's simultaneous presence under a towel.

2. SAMMY'S GLASS EYE BECOMES SINATRA'S KEY RING!

TABLOID Those of you with only passing knowledge of Rat Pack lore may not know that charter member Sammy Davis, Jr., lost an eye in a 1954 car accident. He purchased a glass substitute but never loaned it to Frank Sinatra for any purpose.

3. CASINO GUARD DOGS PROTECT DEANO FROM JERRY LEWIS

TABLOID The acrimonious breakup of the Dean Martin–Jerry Lewis comedy team was one of the biggest entertainment stories of 1956. Despite having appeared together in sixteen hit films, they rarely spoke to each other after the split. Deano found solace with the Rat Pack, and Jerry Lewis became the darling of high-brow French film critics, who, inexplicably, adored his solo films.

4. JOEY BISHOP: "I EMCEED A LION'S CLUB SMUT SHOW"

TABLOID Comedian Joey Bishop starred in a sitcom and even had his own late-night talk show with Regis Philbin as sidekick, but Mr. Bishop never hosted a smoker or strip show at the Lion's Club, VFW Hall, or Moose Lodge.

5. ACTRESS BREAKS LEG TO MAKE SHIRLEY MACLAINE A STAR

TRUTH Before Shirley MacLaine was a New Age guru, she was a Rat Pack gal pal. And before that, she got her first show-business break as an understudy in a musical version of *The Pajama Game*. The star, Carol Haney, actually broke a leg, and Shirley replaced her. After the show, big-time producer Hal Wallis took note of Shirley's talent and signed her to a Hollywood contract.

HEALTH *AND* FITNESS

"Grow Hair and Lose Weight with Wishful Thinking!" "Cry Your Way out of Depression!" "To Achieve Your Dreams, Set Unachievable Goals!"

Don't be surprised if the local newspaper's health-and-fitness section is filled with similarly curious claims. Researchers know that novelty is the key to getting ink about their efforts to improve our physical and emotional well-being. So they engage in many dubious projects to enlighten and, yes, entertain us. That's what can make it difficult to separate truthful health-and-fitness headlines from tabloid whoppers. Can you?

GAME 1

Are the following headlines **TRUTH *or* TABLOID?**
(See next page for correct answers.)

1. **MOTHERHOOD MAKES YOU SMARTER**

2. **MORNING SICKNESS KEEPS YOU HEALTHY**

3. **TO IMPROVE BABY'S VISION, EAT SARDINES WHEN PREGNANT**

4. **TO BETTER BABY'S HEARING, GOBBLE HERRING WHEN EXPECTING**

5. **IF YOU WANT A BOY, EAT VEGETABLES**

1. MOTHERHOOD MAKES YOU SMARTER

TABLOID This is unproven so far, at least for human-type moms, although it does do the trick for mice. A study of female mice found that giving birth made them more curious, prone to fewer mistakes, and able to learn mazes more quickly.

2. MORNING SICKNESS KEEPS YOU HEALTHY

TRUTH So go ahead and throw up. According to Cornell University researchers, the nausea and vomiting of morning sickness protects mother and developing baby from food-borne illnesses and deforming chemicals. The study was based on thousands of pregnancies.

3. TO IMPROVE BABY'S VISION, EAT SARDINES WHEN PREGNANT

TRUTH Researchers at the University of Bristol in England studied the mothers of fourteen thousand children and found that pregnant women who ate oily fish, such as sardines and mackerel, had kids with better visual development. Question: How the heck did they find that many women willing to eat sardines and mackerel for nine months?

4. TO BETTER BABY'S HEARING, GOBBLE HERRING WHEN EXPECTING

TABLOID While scientists have yet to identify which, if any, fish improves hearing, three out of four women agree that they'd rather have morning sickness than eat herring in cream sauce.

5. IF YOU WANT A BOY, EAT VEGETABLES

TABLOID Actually, it's just the opposite. Scientists at Nottingham University in Great Britain have found a way to increase the chances of giving birth to a girl—become a vegetarian. Typically in Britain, 106 boys are born for every 100 girls. But among vegetarian mothers, just 85 boys were born for every 100 girls. Researcher Pauline Hudson suggests that all-veggie diets are more stressful on the body—and the stronger female fetus can survive it, while the weaker male can't.

GAME 2

Are the following headlines **TRUTH** *or* **TABLOID?**
(See next page for correct answers.)

1. "MALE PATTERN VOMITING" LINKED TO COLLEGE ATTENDANCE

2. YOU CAN WORK IN YOUR SLEEP, SAYS EXPERT

3. MORE COMMUTERS CONSULT SHRINK WHILE STUCK IN TRAFFIC

4. CHOCOHOLICS TO GET THEIR OWN "PATCH"

5. BORING PEOPLE LIVE LONGER

And now, for the CORRECT ANSWERS to GAME 2:

1. "MALE PATTERN VOMITING" LINKED TO COLLEGE ATTENDANCE

TABLOID I'm not aware of any such study, but 2 kegs + 50 guys @ 1 party = new carpet pattern.

2. YOU CAN WORK IN YOUR SLEEP, SAYS EXPERT

TRUTH You can make sleeping productive, according to Harvard time-management consultant Alan Lakein. One method: Pose a question to your subsconscious just before you fall asleep. Your mind will have all night to work on the problem. Suggested question #1: "What happened to my life?" Suggested question #2: "Why can't I sleep?"

3. MORE COMMUTERS CONSULT SHRINK WHILE STUCK IN TRAFFIC

TABLOID Although it sounds like a highly efficient time-management technique. By the way, in other traffic news, a study estimates that 750,000 of your fellow drivers are using their car phone at any given moment.

4. CHOCOHOLICS TO GET THEIR OWN "PATCH"

TRUTH A Nicoderm-type skin patch has been tested at St. George's Hospital in London. The patch releases whiffs of vanilla and other scents to help reduce the craving for chocolate. Question: What if someone eats their patch?

5. BORING PEOPLE LIVE LONGER

TABLOID However, like chili burritos with extra salsa and onions, these folks usually remain with you longer and come back when you least expect it.

GAME 3

Are the following headlines **TRUTH** or **TABLOID?**
(See next page for correct answers.)

1. **DRIVING AND THINKING MAY BE HAZARDOUS**

2. **TOO MANY VEGETABLES CAN MAKE YOU BLIND**

3. **ANXIETY AND DEPRESSION ARE GOOD FOR YOU**

4. **SNORING MAKES YOU STUPID**

5. **DARK, STAINED TEETH THE LATEST RAGE**

1. DRIVING AND THINKING MAY BE HAZARDOUS

TRUTH University psychologists in Madrid, Spain, performed an experiment in which drivers were required to think through a verbal task while on the road. The results? According to Dr. L. M. Nunes, "Our research shows for the first time that doing mental calculations while driving may make some people pay less attention to the road and put themselves more at risk for an accident." The surgeon general suggests not thinking for at least one hour before driving. And when driving with others, always appoint a designated thinker.

2. TOO MANY VEGETABLES CAN MAKE YOU BLIND

TRUTH According to French doctors, a thirty-three-year-old man's strict vegetarian diet may have caused him to go blind. The patient had not eaten any form of animal protein for thirteen years when blood tests revealed a deficiency in key vitamins and minerals. By then it was too late to reverse the process that had caused his optic nerves to degenerate. Just think—a single Big Mac might've saved the poor sucker.

3. ANXIETY AND DEPRESSION ARE GOOD FOR YOU

TABLOID This is unfortunate news for fans of losing football teams everywhere.

4. SNORING MAKES YOU STUPID

TRUTH According to the Medica Muelheim clinic in Frankfurt, Germany, snoring kills brain cells by depriving the body of oxygen. A study found that snorers performed worse than nonsnorers in tests of intelligence, reaction time, and eye-hand coordination.

5. DARK, STAINED TEETH THE LATEST RAGE

TABLOID If you are currently in possession of dark, stained teeth, you're about four thousand years too late to be cool. Dark brown or black teeth were popular in Japan four millennia ago, thanks to the practice of decorative tooth-staining called *ohaguro*. There are visual hints, though, that the ancient art has gained favor with the royal family of England.

GAME 4

Are the following headlines **TRUTH** *or* **TABLOID?**
(See next page for correct answers.)

1. To Relieve Chest Pain, Drill Holes In Heart

2. Divorce Is Contagious

3. Researcher Studies Thumbs Of Corpses

4. Suppressing Emotion Makes Your Brain Shrink

5. Ladies! To Increase Sex Appeal, Drink Mountain Dew

1. TO RELIEVE CHEST PAIN, DRILL HOLES IN HEART

TRUTH For unknown reasons, drilling tiny holes in the heart can relieve disabling chest pain, according to findings presented at a 2001 American Heart Association meeting in New Orleans. The benefits of treating patients that way, using a carbon dioxide laser, last at least five years, says Dr. Keith Horvath of Northwestern University Medical Center. Scientists speculate that drilling holes might spur growth proteins and cause the heart muscle to develop new blood vessels, enabling more oxygen to travel throughout the heart, relieving pain.

2. DIVORCE IS CONTAGIOUS

TRUTH At least it is for men. Swedish sociologist Yvonne Aberg surveyed thirty-seven thousand people at fifteen hundred places of work. She found that men were more likely to file for divorce when a male coworker had already done so. Women weren't affected to the same degree. In fact, they often worked harder at their own marriages when a colleague divorced.

3. RESEARCHER STUDIES THUMBS OF CORPSES

TRUTH Francisco Valero-Cuevas, assistant professor of mechanical and aerospace engineering at Cornell University, received a two-hundred-thousand-dollar grant to study thumbs. A device manipulates the thumbs of corpses, allowing the professor to study their range of motion. Hopefully, over time, the result will be improved hitchhiking techniques.

4. SUPPRESSING EMOTION MAKES YOUR BRAIN SHRINK

TABLOID But keeping emotions bottled up does interfere with your ability to think clearly and remember details. Denying your real feelings creates a distraction, causing you to be less observant about the world around you, say Stanford University researchers. Which is why guys can't remember the plotline of any movie featuring Jennifer Lopez.

5. LADIES! TO INCREASE SEX APPEAL, DRINK MOUNTAIN DEW

TABLOID One guy to another: "Boy, that gal is purty. And that dang filly sure can handle her Mountain Dew!"

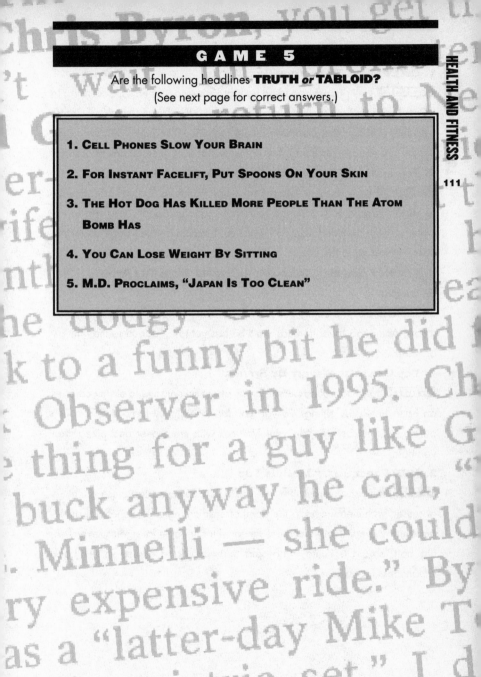

GAME 5

Are the following headlines **TRUTH or TABLOID?**
(See next page for correct answers.)

1. CELL PHONES SLOW YOUR BRAIN

2. FOR INSTANT FACELIFT, PUT SPOONS ON YOUR SKIN

3. THE HOT DOG HAS KILLED MORE PEOPLE THAN THE ATOM BOMB HAS

4. YOU CAN LOSE WEIGHT BY SITTING

5. M.D. PROCLAIMS, "JAPAN IS TOO CLEAN"

1. CELL PHONES SLOW YOUR BRAIN

TABLOID Cell phones speed up your brain's response times, according to a British expert. Biophysicist Dr. Alan Preece of the Bristol Oncology Center said that six separate studies indicate that response times quicken when people are exposed to the radio-frequency signals from their cell phones.

2. FOR INSTANT FACELIFT, PUT SPOONS ON YOUR SKIN

TRUTH Berlin beauty expert Rene Kock maintains that you can achieve an instant facelift with common household spoons. Spoons warmed in hot water smooth wrinkled skin, while ice-cold spoons reduce bags under the eyes, according to Kock.

3. THE HOT DOG HAS KILLED MORE PEOPLE THAN THE ATOM BOMB HAS

TABLOID Despite being stuffed with an ever-changing variety of mystery meats, America's favorite meal-in-a-tube has yet to be added to the military arsenal.

4. YOU CAN LOSE WEIGHT BY SITTING

TRUTH A 150-pound person burns about seventy-five to eighty calories an hour merely by sitting. So you can lose weight by becoming a couch potato, as long as you don't stuff yourself with more beer and pizza than you burn.

5. M.D. PROCLAIMS, "JAPAN IS TOO CLEAN"

TRUTH Dr. Koichiro Fujita, a.k.a. Dr. Dirt, says that Japanese society is obsessed with cleanliness to the point of eradicating even beneficial bacteria. Nearly every item in Japan is laced with antibacterial agents, even fishing bait, says Dr. Fujita, who sold thirty thousand copies of his book *Cleanliness Is Sickness*.

GAME 6

Are the following headlines **TRUTH** *or* **TABLOID**?
(See next page for correct answers.)

1. STRESSED? COAT YOUR BODY WITH BBQ SAUCE

2. WATCHING TV MOVIES CAN RUIN YOUR LIFE

3. DURING COLD SEASON, YOU MAKE 10 GALLONS OF SNOT

4. SNOTTY HEALTH CLUB EXPELS WOMEN OVER SIZE 8

5. TO BEAT JET LAG, WEAR FUZZY SLIPPERS

TRUTH or TABLOID?

1. STRESSED? COAT YOUR BODY WITH BBQ SAUCE

TRUTH The exclusive Crescent Court Hotel in Dallas offers a calming spa treatment that includes a cosmetic barbecue sauce "wrap." The mixture of honey, tomato paste, and secret spices is spread on the client's skin as she snoozes peacefully. (After which she's skewered and cooked rotisserie-style over a glowing pit of charcoal briquettes.)

114

2. WATCHING TV MOVIES CAN RUIN YOUR LIFE

TABLOID Among other benefits, issue-oriented TV movies help teach about problems you may one day face. They also show that you're not alone in having troubles, says Dr. Elayne Rapping, professor of communications at Adelphi University in New York. However, watching a TV movie that stars Kathie Lee Gifford can definitely ruin your day.

3. DURING COLD SEASON, YOU MAKE 10 GALLONS OF SNOT

TABLOID It only feels like it.

4. SNOTTY HEALTH CLUB EXPELS WOMEN OVER SIZE 8

TABLOID That would be cruel and unusual punishment, even for an establishment that makes you run in place until you're ready to pass out.

5. TO BEAT JET LAG, WEAR FUZZY SLIPPERS

TRUTH Sleeping on planes is difficult because we can't get completely horizontal, say researchers. Our bodies respond to the strange semireclining position by constricting the blood vessels in the legs. This keeps our core body temperature from dropping enough to induce restful sleep. Anything that encourages blood vessels in the feet to dilate will help foster much-needed sleep—like warm, fuzzy slippers.

GAME 7

Are the following headlines **TRUTH** *or* **TABLOID**?
(See next page for correct answers.)

1. **BARBIE DOLLS ARE SICKENING**

2. **RIDING ROLLERCOASTERS LOWERS IQ**

3. **MEAT EATERS HAVE BETTER MARRIAGES**

4. **TOFU MAKES YOU STUPID**

5. **ANNOYED WITH YOUR MATE? VISUALIZE HIM NAKED**

1. BARBIE DOLLS ARE SICKENING

TABLOID In truth, it's that lovable little teddy bear that can be a health hazard. Concerned health officials at Christchurch School of Medicine in New Zealand say that 90 percent of teddy bears possess moderate to heavy bacterial contamination, a result of being handled by sick children. The pathogens can be passed on to healthy children who play with the bears, causing them to become ill. Soft toys like teddy bears are more difficult to disinfect than hard toys like Barbie dolls, and they quickly get recontaminated after cleaning. "Isn't it time to give teddy the boot?" asks Christchurch spokesperson Paul Corwin.

2. RIDING ROLLERCOASTERS LOWERS IQ

TABLOID No such evidence yet. In 2001, three rollercoaster riders suffered brain hemorrhages, two of them fatal. However, safety officials found no relation between the rides and the injuries. So, enjoy!

3. MEAT EATERS HAVE BETTER MARRIAGES

TABLOID Did you know, however, that one way to feel better about your spouse is to see a happy movie? A researcher interviewed moviegoers after they watched either a happy or a sad movie. People who viewed the happy movie were more positive about their marriage. People who saw the sad one filed for divorce before the end credits. (Just kidding, three-hankie-film fans.)

4. TOFU MAKES YOU STUPID

TRUTH Time to celebrate, steak fans! In a study published by the Hawaii Center for Health Research, men who ate the most tofu during their mid-forties to mid-sixties showed the most signs of mental decline thirty years later. The more tofu eaten, the greater the likelihood of mental deterioration, according to lead researcher Dr. Lon White. The study tracked the health of more than forty-five hundred men, beginning in 1965.

5. ANNOYED WITH YOUR MATE? VISUALIZE HIM NAKED

TABLOID Not quite. Instead, envision your partner wrapped in a white light when you're feeling critical of him. That's the advice of Dr. Paul Coleman, a marriage and family expert, who says that this technique helps you to stifle your petty irritations. Like when he "forgets" to bathe for a week.

GAME 8

Are the following headlines **TRUTH** *or* **TABLOID?**
(See next page for correct answers.)

1. **POLLUTED MEN FATHER MORE BOYS**

2. **THE MORE YOU SWEAT, THE MORE YOU LEARN**

3. **TO FEEL PLEASURE, POUND YOUR HAND WITH A HAMMER**

4. **HEALTH NUTS ADD LIQUID DNA TO SMOOTHIES**

5. **CRIMINALS "PROFILED" BY SIZE OF PENIS**

And now, for the CORRECT ANSWERS to GAME 8:

1. POLLUTED MEN FATHER MORE BOYS

TRUTH Hey, guys! If your dream is to father an NFL quarterback or NBA center, consider increasing the amount of PCB in your blood. Researchers at Michigan State University discovered that men with higher blood levels of the polluting chemicals known as PCBs fathered a greater percentage of boys. Their study found that 57 percent of the children of high-PCB men were males, while unpolluted men had boys only 51 percent of the time.

2. THE MORE YOU SWEAT, THE MORE YOU LEARN

TABLOID In fact, Boston University psychologists say you can learn without even trying, let alone breaking into a sweat. Participants in a complex study improved their scores considerably despite an interval of twenty-five days between the first and second time they took the same test, which shows that they were processing information even when not actively trying to.

3. TO FEEL PLEASURE, POUND YOUR HAND WITH A HAMMER

TRUTH University of California at San Francisco scientists have determined that inducing pain—like accidentally hitting your hand with a hammer—initiates a chemical process that, oddly enough, helps to relieve your suffering. This long-lasting relief is produced by the brain's "reward" pathway, the same network that prompts pleasurable feelings in response to certain behaviors, like quenching your thirst and having sex.

4. HEALTH NUTS ADD LIQUID DNA TO SMOOTHIES

TABLOID Hasn't happened yet, but scientists at the University of North Carolina at Chapel Hill have figured out how to create DNA in liquid form. "It's the consistency of honey in wintertime Vermont," according to chemistry professor Royce W. Murray.

5. CRIMINALS "PROFILED" BY SIZE OF PENIS

TABLOID No relationship has been found between penis size and criminal activity. But health officials in India recently measured twenty-one hundred penises throughout the nation in order to see if government-issued condoms should vary in size according to region. There had been an increase in complaints of condoms breaking under use.

GAME 9

Are the following headlines **TRUTH** *or* **TABLOID?**
(See next page for correct answers.)

1. CELL PHONES HELP TEENS KICK CIGARETTES

2. TO FEEL SMARTER, BRUSH YOUR TEETH

3. RUGGED INDIVIDUALISTS ARE MISERABLE

4. ICE CREAM IS GOOD FOR YOU

5. PLAGUED BY GHOSTS? THIS SUPPORT GROUP CAN HELP

1. CELL PHONES HELP TEENS KICK CIGARETTES

TRUTH According to researcher Anne Charlton of the University of Manchester in England, the rise in cell-phone use is related to a decline in teen smoking. "The marketing of mobile phones is rooted in promoting self-image and identity, which resembles cigarette advertising," she says. Charlton adds that many teens can't afford both habits and prefer the high-tech kick of cell phones, which allows them to connect with friends on the move. In other words, British teens can't talk and smoke at the same time.

2. TO FEEL SMARTER, BRUSH YOUR TEETH

TABLOID However, a Yale University study does conclude that people feel smarter, more capable, and even more sociable when their hair is neat and combed. Researchers questioned 120 ordinary folks and learned that men feel even more out of sorts on a bad-hair day than women do.

3. RUGGED INDIVIDUALISTS ARE MISERABLE

TABLOID Quite the contrary. Having a sense of personal autonomy is the number-1 quality that makes people happy, according to a University of Missouri study. Participants ranked the need to be in control of one's own destiny as the most important of ten basic psychological needs—including close social relationships.

4. ICE CREAM IS GOOD FOR YOU

TRUTH The good news: Eating three to four servings a day of low-fat ice cream can enhance weight loss. The bad news: The research was conducted on laboratory mice. However, researchers did conclude that calcium stored in human fat cells plays a key role in causing the eventual breakdown of that fat. I'm looking forward to the "Cherry Garcia Diet."

5. PLAGUED BY GHOSTS? THIS SUPPORT GROUP CAN HELP

TRUTH The Capital Ghost Forum, headquartered in Pennsylvania, runs support groups for folks who've seen ghosts. Founded in 1996, the organization is "like an Alcoholics Anonymous for people who have ghosts," says spokesperson Kelly Weaver. She says that most individuals who attend meetings are curious, though a bit frightened at first. But by telling their story to others who are hounded by ghosts, they feel reassured that they're not alone.

GAME 10

Are the following headlines **TRUTH or TABLOID?**
(See next page for correct answers.)

1. SNEEZING CAN PREVENT CONCEIVING

2. MONOGAMY: HISTORY'S MOST CONDEMNED SEX PRACTICE

3. PSYCHOTICS SPEND $5 BILLION A YEAR

4. FRENCHMAN TRAINS NOSE TO IDENTIFY 800 SCENTS

5. COUPLES SHOULD FIGHT STANDING UP

1. SNEEZING CAN PREVENT CONCEIVING

TABLOID Yet, a physician in ancient Greece suggested this bizarre method to avoid conception. He advised that after lovemaking, women climb out of bed, sit down with bended knees, and make themselves sneeze repeatedly.

2. MONOGAMY: HISTORY'S MOST CONDEMNED SEX PRACTICE

TABLOID Actually, the winner of that contest is masturbation. Throughout history, the supposed consequences of "self-abuse" have included vertigo, loss of memory, hysteria, asthma, mania, dementia, paralysis—and even death!

3. PSYCHOTICS SPEND $5 BILLION A YEAR

TRUTH Amazingly, the seriously mentally ill are now coughing up $5 billion a year on drugs to treat their disorders. Two major drug companies are engaged in an all-out war to dominate the fast-growing market, leading to a slew of bitter accusations. Pfizer, for instance, claims that Eli Lilly's antipsychotic Zyprexa makes users fat. Lilly hints that Pfizer's new Geodon may kill patients.

4. FRENCHMAN TRAINS NOSE TO IDENTIFY 800 SCENTS

TRUTH Roja Dove, forty-four, travels the world for the French perfume company Guerlain, instructing women about fragrance. He claims to have taught his own nose to identify eight hundred different perfume scents. Dove started collecting perfume bottles at the age of eighteen. For more than twenty-five years, he's worn Guerlain's Mitsouko, a spicy women's perfume.

5. COUPLES SHOULD FIGHT STANDING UP

TABLOID In fact, when an argument starts, the best thing to do is to sit down—together. According to marriage therapists, remaining seated while talking reduces the risk of intimidating postures and premature exits, and emotions flare more easily when people are standing.

BUSINESS

Light a Cuban cigar, pour two fingers of brandy, don your power suit, and start thinking like a boss, because this chapter means business, and the buck, dear reader, stops with you. Yes, the business section is where money talks, bull**** walks, and you'll be removed from further responsibilities as a Truth or Tabloid? player if you don't rack up a good score. Your challenge is clear: Determine when, like Enron's quarterly reports, some headlines are too good to be true.

GAME 1

Are the following headlines **TRUTH or TABLOID?**
(See next page for correct answers.)

1. **A NUDIST INVENTED THE LAVA LAMP**

2. **INVENTOR CREATES PORTABLE LAWN FOR HOMESICK TRAVELERS**

3. **GROSS! FREQUENT FLIER MILES—FOR THE DEAD**

4. **RALPH LAUREN COPS PRISON UNIFORM CONTRACT**

5. **EMPLOYEE SEVERANCE PAY INCLUDES 7,000 BOTTLES OF BEER**

1. A NUDIST INVENTED THE LAVA LAMP

TRUTH Edward Craven Walker was a devoted nudist who launched the Lava Lamp in 1963, after a ten-year struggle to perfect the weird oil-and-water device. It became popular in the sixties, during the way-out "psychedelic" craze. Mr. Walker, who died at age eighty-two, also produced the 1950s nudie movies *Eves on Skis* and *Traveling Light,* which featured nude underwater dancing.

2. INVENTOR CREATES PORTABLE LAWN FOR HOMESICK TRAVELERS

TABLOID Right, he also created pop-up shrubs and papier-mâché neighbors who dissolve in the rain.

3. GROSS! FREQUENT FLIER MILES—FOR THE DEAD

TRUTH Funeral directors who ship coffins on Delta Air Lines receive frequent flier miles from Daytona International Airport in Florida. For every coffin flown, five hundred frequent flier miles are awarded. Apparently, shipping coffins is particularly lucrative in central Florida. For many years, thousands of the dearly departed have been shipped back to their cold and snowy hometowns in other regions of the United States.

4. RALPH LAUREN COPS PRISON UNIFORM CONTRACT

TABLOID Could an improved wardrobe, however, reduce recidivism among hardened cons whose self-esteem has been crushed after an entire sentence spent in a baggy orange jumpsuit? Just a thought.

5. EMPLOYEE SEVERANCE PAY INCLUDES 7,000 BOTTLES OF BEER

TRUTH Workers at a closing Guinness plant in Ireland agreed to a severance package that included ten years of free beer. Each eligible employee received about fourteen free bottles of Guinness per week, plus extra on holidays, for a total of more than seven thousand bottles. Oh, yeah, they also got up to $150,000 apiece.

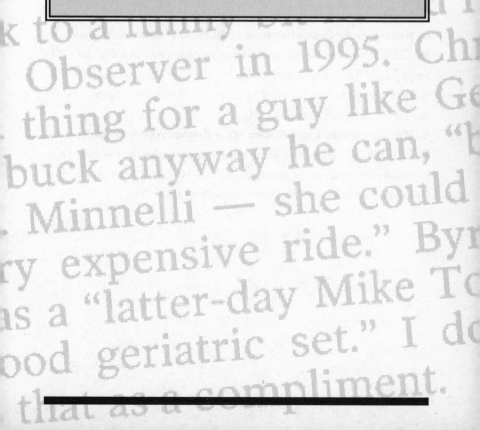

GAME 2

Are the following headlines **TRUTH** *or* **TABLOID?**
(See next page for correct answers.)

1. LAP DANCERS TIGHTEN BELTS AS PATRONS' PAYCHECKS SHRINK

2. VEGETARIAN CLAIMS HEALTH DAMAGED BY "SECONDHAND MEAT"

3. CLUB MED OPENS RESORT FOR RETIRED SWINGERS

4. HERSHEY'S SUES DERMATOLOGIST OVER ANTI-CHOCOLATE AD

5. HERSHEY HOTEL FILLS ROOMS WITH CHOCOLATE-COVERED GUESTS

1. Lap Dancers Tighten Belts As Patrons' Paychecks Shrink

TRUTH A survey of exotic dance clubs on the Internet has uncovered the disturbing news. A lap dance, a form of adult entertainment that used to be worth thirty to forty dollars during boom times, can now be had for as little as five bucks during happy hour at select establishments.

2. Vegetarian Claims Health Damaged By "Secondhand Meat"

TRUTH A vegetarian at an outdoor festival in downtown Eugene, Oregon, complained about the pervasive smell of grilled chicken wafting from food stalls. A food columnist in the heavily New Age community agreed that steps needed to be taken to "protect us all from secondhand meat in the future."

3. Club Med Opens Resort For Retired Swingers

TABLOID Too bad, because it would be nice to see a retirement home with rules like "No loud sex during nap hour" and "Early-bird orgies begin at 4:30 P.M."

4. Hershey's Sues Dermatologist Over Anti-Chocolate Ad

TABLOID Maybe the ad could have started something like this: "My name is Sid Fark. I'm a dermatologist, and every morning another tormented teen slinks into my waiting room, his or her face ravaged by the uncontrolled consumption of chocolate."

5. Hershey Hotel Fills Rooms With Chocolate-Covered Guests

TRUTH The multimillion-dollar spa at Hotel Hershey in Hershey, Pennsylvania, allows pampered guests to coat their bodies in chocolate "mud"—chocolate mud baths and chocolate cosmetic wraps.

GAME 3

Are the following headlines **TRUTH** *or* **TABLOID?**
(See next page for correct answers.)

1. MORE WORKERS CONDUCT BUSINESS IN BATHROOMS

2. NOW YOU CAN ENJOY DELICIOUS CARBONATED PEARS

3. ATHEIST SUES EMPLOYER FOR CELEBRATING CHRISTMAS

4. INVENTOR OF CHILLED FORK AWARDED CULINARY "OSCAR"

5. OPTICIAN CREATES BRAILLE EYE CHART

127

1. MORE WORKERS CONDUCT BUSINESS IN BATHROOMS

TRUTH The rest room has replaced the traditional break room as a place where workers informally exchange ideas. Business architects have responded by redesigning and enlarging rest rooms to enhance employee interaction. "If the bathrooms can do this while providing a safe and comfortable environment, then why not make them better?" asks UCLA architecture professor Barton Myers.

One beleaguered employee to another: "Would you look at this? The boss's stall is bigger than my cubicle."

2. NOW YOU CAN ENJOY DELICIOUS CARBONATED PEARS

TRUTH Galen Kaufman, professor of neuroscience at the University of Texas, has created what he calls the Fizzyfruit. It's a process that adds carbonation to any fruit containing more than 80 percent water, including pears, strawberries, and grapes. The process also works with certain vegetables. By the way, Dr. Kaufman writes science fiction novels in his spare time, none of which is titled *Honey, I Carbonated the Kids!*

3. ATHEIST SUES EMPLOYER FOR CELEBRATING CHRISTMAS

TABLOID However, in one northwestern community, the city manager banned Christmas trees from public buildings to ensure that no visitors would be "offended" by their presence. After a resounding uproar from the citizenry, he reversed his position a year later.

4. INVENTOR OF CHILLED FORK AWARDED CULINARY "OSCAR"

TABLOID The creator of this milestone in utensil use has yet to be recognized. But the chilled fork, which many thought became extinct years ago, still thrives at certain fine-dining establishments. Spring Mill Manor in prestigious Bucks County, Pennsylvania, even advertised that "white-glove service, chilled forks, and glorious food presentations are all standard here at the manor."

5. OPTICIAN CREATES BRAILLE EYE CHART

TABLOID She will, however, give you a discount on your second pair of eyeglasses, whether you need them or not.

GAME 4

Are the following headlines **TRUTH *or* TABLOID?**
(See next page for correct answers.)

1. **INSURANCE POLICY COVERS ALIEN ABDUCTIONS**

2. **WATCHING CARS BLOW UP SPIKES SALES**

3. **MORE ROLLS-ROYCES RECALLED THAN DAEWOOS**

4. **YOU CAN GET FIRED FOR SWEARING**

5. **MORE EMPLOYEES REQUIRED TO WORK WHILE ON VACATION**

And now, for the CORRECT ANSWERS to GAME 4:

1. INSURANCE POLICY COVERS ALIEN ABDUCTIONS

TRUTH Goodfellows, a London insurer, has sold about fifty thousand policies that compensate victims in the event that they are abducted by UFO aliens. The policies range in cost, starting at $150, and offer roughly $1.5 million coverage against abduction or impregnation by aliens. To file a claim, policyholders must present photographic or visual evidence, pass a lie detector test, and have a reliable third-party witness, preferably from Earth.

2. WATCHING CARS BLOW UP SPIKES SALES

TRUTH Car manufacturers from Ford to Audi say that vehicles smashed, burned, or blown up in movies often experience a spurt in sales soon after. The small imports raced and wrecked in the film *The Fast and the Furious* are examples.

3. MORE ROLLS-ROYCES RECALLED THAN DAEWOOS

TABLOID Sometimes, though, even Rolls-Royce owners can be subjected to the indignity of a car recalled for repair. In fact, the company recalled *five* models recently, including the Corniche. An extension pipe needed to be added to vent gas vapors in the deluxe vehicles. The company became aware of the flaw when one $360,000 Corniche exploded after electric currents from power windows ignited vapors built up during fueling.

4. YOU CAN GET FIRED FOR SWEARING

TRUTH The Michigan Court of Appeals found that the Farmer Jack supermarket chain was justified in firing a bagger with Tourette's syndrome who cursed uncontrollably in front of customers.

Bagger to customer: "Would you like #$%^ plastic or *&^%$ paper?"

5. MORE EMPLOYEES REQUIRED TO WORK WHILE ON VACATION

TABLOID An eye-opening survey by the American Management Association did find that 26 percent of executives planned to contact their offices daily while vacationing. Only 31 percent said they'd take the traditional two weeks off. Most wanted to divide their vacations into smaller portions instead.

GAME 5

Are the following headlines **TRUTH** *or* **TABLOID?**
(See next page for correct answers.)

1. **DOT ON FOREHEAD TO REPLACE COMPUTER MOUSE**

2. **BIG CORPORATE PUSH TO STOP BELCHING COWS**

3. **ACTIVISTS FREE MILLIONS OF SILK-PRODUCING WORMS**

4. **HIGHWAY CREATES ITS OWN BAD WEATHER**

5. **NEW "PATCH" TO CONTROL FAT CRAVINGS**

1. DOT ON FOREHEAD TO REPLACE COMPUTER MOUSE

TRUTH If techno whiz Jim Richardson has his way, the Naturalpoint TrackIR will become a common sight on desktops everywhere. Here's how it works: A user affixes a disposable dot to her forehead or glasses. A device containing four LEDs and a camera is plugged into her computer. The LEDs shine an invisible beam of light on the dot. As the user moves her head, the camera and the tracker's software cause a pointer to travel across the computer monitor, much like a mouse does.

2. BIG CORPORATE PUSH TO STOP BELCHING COWS

TRUTH Apparently, it's not just mad cow disease we should worry about. TransAlta, Canada's largest private power company, has entered into a pact to reduce belching and flatulence in livestock. Why? Methane gas emanating from cows is believed to play a major part in global warming.

3. ACTIVISTS FREE MILLIONS OF SILK-PRODUCING WORMS

TABLOID As you read this, no doubt countless silkworms are still being exploited throughout the world by a ruthless international cartel of scarf manufacturers. Will it ever end?

4. HIGHWAY CREATES ITS OWN BAD WEATHER

TRUTH Created as a result of the Federal Intermodal Surface Transportation Efficiency Act in 1991, the Smart Road in Blacksburg, Virginia, looks pretty much like any other four-lane highway. But seventy-five weather towers are positioned along the five-mile winding road, spewing up to two inches of rain or four inches of snow per hour onto the road surface, which helps engineers evaluate the impact of severe weather on various types of pavement. However, some suspect the road was actually created as a result of the Federal Full Employment for Civil Engineers Who Like Big Toys Act.

5. NEW "PATCH" TO CONTROL FAT CRAVINGS

TABLOID If Nicoderm can make a patch for smokers, why not one for people addicted to bacon cheeseburgers and the like? Or how about a patch for bad dates? You know—slap a patch on the morning after, forget who you were with the night before.

GAME 6

Are the following headlines **TRUTH** *or* **TABLOID?**
(See next page for correct answers.)

1. **TO GET AHEAD, GET FIRED**

2. **TRENDY SIBERIA IS NEW HIGH-TECH HAVEN**

3. **PROSTHETIC DOG TESTICLES END NEUTERING SHAME**

4. **BOSS PROMOTES ONLY BLONDES, CHARGES BRUNETTE**

5. **OXYGEN BAR ADDS WATER AND SUNLIGHT**

TRUTH or TABLOID?

1. To Get Ahead, Get Fired

TRUTH Getting fired can be a ringing reminder that you and your job aren't the right fit, according to experts. You're freed to find something more in line with your skills instead of getting mired for years in a position you hate. And you're much more likely to move up the ladder doing work you perform well. Feel better now?

134

2. Trendy Siberia Is New High-Tech Haven

TRUTH Russian nerds are flocking to the frozen tundra in search of fame and fortune. The city of Novosibirsk, dubbed "Siberia's Silicon Valley," is now home to fifteen thousand scientists and researchers, five thousand students, and twenty-five software companies. Programmers earn up to fifteen hundred dollars a month in a region where doctors are paid twenty-five dollars a week.

3. Prosthetic Dog Testicles End Neutering Shame

TRUTH That's the claim for Neuticals, prosthetic dog testicles that are surgically implanted after neutering. The company that manufactures them says that a pet can suffer from "postneutering trauma" because he's missing a "familiar body part." They cost $30 to $130 a pair, depending on size.

4. Boss Promotes Only Blondes, Charges Brunette

TABLOID Brunette to boss: "What do I need to get ahead in this %&$* company?"

Boss to brunette: "Clairol Summer Blonde."

5. Oxygen Bar Adds Water And Sunlight

TABLOID Oxygen bars are having it tough, even when they try to extend the product line. A husband-and-wife team lost their life savings when their Pacific Northwest oxygen bar closed after six weeks in business. Of course, that may have something to do with the fact that air quality in their community is about as good as it gets, short of pure oxygen.

GAME 7

Are the following headlines **TRUTH** *or* **TABLOID?**
(See next page for correct answers.)

1. To Keep Fit, Pretend Your Desk Is A Ballet Bar

2. New "Gassy" Telephone F*rts Instead Of Rings

3. Dairy Farmer Connects Herd To His Computer

4. Republicans Are Better Tippers, Say Lap Dancers

5. Doc To Execs: To De-Stress Life, Become A Secretary

1. To Keep Fit, Pretend Your Desk Is A Ballet Bar

TRUTH According to Judi Sheppard Missett, CEO of Jazzercise, one way to exercise at work is to use your desk as a ballet bar. Simply lift your leg forward, to the side, and then back ten times to give your leg muscles a workout. Just be sure to wear pants, she warns.

2. New "Gassy" Telephone F*rts Instead Of Rings

TRUTH According to the sales pitch, you can "amaze family and friends with the world's first f*rting phone. It works like a regular phone— except for the di-stink-tive ringer. Just plug it into any standard wall jack. You can switch from f*rt to normal ring whenever you feel like it."

3. Dairy Farmer Connects Herd To His Computer

TRUTH Mike Pank, a dairy farmer in upstate New York, has attached small radio transmitters to the legs of hundreds of his cows. The transmitters send data to the computer system in his office, telling him how many steps each cow takes every day. Why does he care so much? A cow that doesn't move much may be sick and in need of veterinary care. A cow's activity is also linked to her estrous cycle. A high degree of activity indicates that she's ready to be bred.

4. Republicans Are Better Tippers, Say Lap Dancers

TABLOID But beware, politicians. Data is still being gathered.

5. Doc To Execs: To De-Stress Life, Become A Secretary

TABLOID Although many executives do work under lots of pressure, they have a sense of control over how they deal with their workload—delegating certain projects, for example. Secretaries and other clerical workers experience a great deal more stress. Their pace of work is usually set by their bosses, and they labor long hours for low pay and little recognition. Not surprisingly, they also have a high rate of heart disease.

GAME 8

Are the following headlines **TRUTH** *or* **TABLOID?**
(See next page for correct answers.)

1. **To Motivate Employees, Treat Them Like Children**

2. **To Achieve Success, Just Do Your Damn Job**

3. **Sex Store Declares National Orgasm Day**

4. **Nudist Camp Security Guard Must Also Be Naked**

5. **Buyers Of New Ferrari Must Promise Not To Sell It**

1. To Motivate Employees, Treat Them Like Children

TABLOID In fact, expecting a lot from your employees usually reaps great rewards, says Bob Nelson, an author and expert on the workplace. Nelson points out that employees on the lowest rungs of the organization often produce the best ideas, such as the gutsy Starbucks worker who created and served a Frappuccino, even when her boss ordered her not to.

2. To Achieve Success, Just Do Your Damn Job

TABLOID The truth is that you're more likely to achieve greater rewards at work—including a promotion and a bigger paycheck—when you exceed your job description. According to employment experts, employers want folks who take initiative, size up situations, and do what needs to be done.

Employee: "But I'm already doing the work of three people!"

Boss: "Ah, yes, but can you do that in consecutive eight-hour shifts?"

3. Sex Store Declares National Orgasm Day

TRUTH A British sex-store chain recently declared National Orgasm Day, based on the results of a survey that found that 80 percent of British women faked orgasm.

4. Nudist Camp Security Guard Must Also Be Naked

TABLOID By the way, the biggest danger to business at the Helios Nudist Association near Edmonton, Alberta, is mosquitoes. Around dusk, the bugs become so thick that nudists must huddle together near smoky fires. And wear bug spray—everywhere.

5. Buyers Of New Ferrari Must Promise Not To Sell It

TRUTH When a rich guy plunks down $250,000 for a Ferrari, he can often resell it for a huge profit as soon as the ink dries on the contract. The reason? So few exotic Ferraris are built that they're treated more like fine-art collectibles than transportation. To prevent quick reselling by speculators, Ferrari of North America required buyers of its limited-edition 550 Barchetta Pininfarina to sign a document stating that for the first twelve months, they'd offer the dealer first rights to buy the car back at no more than full price.

GAME 9

Are the following headlines **TRUTH** *or* **TABLOID?**

(See next page for correct answers.)

1. TRUCK STOP ADDS MOVIE THEATER

2. SNOOPY MICROCHIP MEASURES HOW MUCH BARTENDER POURS

3. EXPERT: WRITE YOUR RÉSUMÉ LIKE A STEPHEN KING NOVEL

4. IMPRESS INTERVIEWERS BY PLAYING HARD-TO-GET

5. GETTING PISSED AT YOUR BOSS CAN BE GOOD FOR YOU

1. TRUCK STOP ADDS MOVIE THEATER

TRUTH Competition between truck stops has become fierce, according to Parry Desmond, editor of the trucking magazine *Commercial Carrier Journal*. So they've added more creature comforts, like hair salons, food courts, and arcades. The Jubitz Truck Stop in Oregon topped everybody by opening an eighty-seat movie theater.

"Lissen up, rubber duckies. Let's get a convoy goin' to Jubitz. They got a new thirty-five-mm print of *Smokey and the Bandit 3*."

2. SNOOPY MICROCHIP MEASURES HOW MUCH BARTENDER POURS

TRUTH A service called the Beverage Tracker places a microchip in liquor bottle spouts to monitor the exact size of every shot your friendly bartender pours. The information is transmitted wirelessly to a database so that the bar owner can match it against cash register receipts.

3. EXPERT: WRITE YOUR RÉSUMÉ LIKE A STEPHEN KING NOVEL

TABLOID The best résumés are simple and straightforward, with no bells or whistles, unlike:

My Résumé

Position Desired: Vampire

Work Experience: From 1387 to 1398, I was affiliated with Prince Vlad Charnel House, Inc., of Transylvania, Romania, working on antidotes for garlic and wolfbane. From 1401 through present, I freelanced for a variety of distinguished evil entities and prominent undead.

Salary Requirements: three small warm-blooded animals daily and a satin-lined coffin with creaky hinges.

See—straightforward and to the point.

4. IMPRESS INTERVIEWERS BY PLAYING HARD-TO-GET

TABLOID Interviewer: "I like you. Can you start Friday night?"
Interviewee: "Gee, I'm busy. How about Monday for coffee?"

5. GETTING PISSED AT YOUR BOSS CAN BE GOOD FOR YOU

TRUTH "Anger is basically good because of the information it provides," according to psychologist Hendrie Weisinger, author of the book *Emotional Intelligence at Work*.

GAME 10

Are the following headlines **TRUTH** *or* **TABLOID**?
(See next page for correct answers.)

1. **MAKE BIG MONEY SWATTING THE RIGHT KIND OF FLIES**

2. **YOUR DREAM JOB IS THE ONE YOU'VE GOT**

3. **PLAY GOLF IN BATHROOM WITH THE "POTTY PUTTER"**

4. **IT'S HERE! LIPSTICK WITH CONTRACEPTIVES**

5. **RUSSIAN INCOME TAX CAN BE HIGHER THAN INCOME!**

1. MAKE BIG MONEY SWATTING THE RIGHT KIND OF FLIES

TABLOID Interestingly enough, though, you can profit from another beer-guzzling front-porch pursuit—guessing the temperature. The Chicago Mercantile Exchange now offers trading in weather futures and options—financial instruments that are based on the average daily temperatures in major cities across the United States.

2. YOUR DREAM JOB IS THE ONE YOU'VE GOT

TRUTH Having a "dream job" is more a matter of your attitude than the actual position you occupy, according to business consultant and author Richard C. Whiteley. Which is why it's a better idea to learn how to enjoy your current job than flee to a new one. It should come as no great shock that the title of Whiteley's book is *Love the Work You're With*.

3. PLAY GOLF IN BATHROOM WITH THE "POTTY PUTTER"

TRUTH Here's a clever game to fight bathroom boredom. The Potty Putter is a toy fabric golf green, complete with hole, flag, ball, and putter. The inventor says golf enthusiasts can put the game on the floor and play while, *ahem*, sitting on the bowl.

4. IT'S HERE! LIPSTICK WITH CONTRACEPTIVES

TABLOID Not quite, but upscale Elizabeth Arden created Lip, Lip Hooray with the toothpaste ingredient zinc citrate. It dissolves when wet to kill odor in saliva.

Gal to guy: "I'd like to kiss you, but I haven't brushed my lips yet."

5. RUSSIAN INCOME TAX CAN BE HIGHER THAN INCOME!

TRUTH The antiquated Russian tax system is so out of whack that taxes can total more than 100 percent, which is just one reason why so many businesses hide their earnings and the government constantly flirts with bankruptcy.

ARTS *AND*
ENTERTAINMENT

What's a singer to do when they pull the plug on the karaoke machine? The same thing a desperate entertainment reporter does when that great big star refuses to be interviewed: He improvises. Can you tell the difference between improv and real in these headlines about all things show biz, from the garage band that was asphyxiated by car fumes to the comedian who was assaulted by fourteen thousand pies over his long and distinguished career?

GAME 1

Are the following headlines **TRUTH or TABLOID?**
(See next page for correct answers.)

1. **ALL-STAR LINEUP TO "RAP" THE BIBLE**

2. **MAGICIAN FAKES OWN CREMATION**

3. **NEW FOR COUCH POTATOES! ORGANIC TV DINNERS**

4. **GRATEFUL DEAD CD TO FEATURE LARGE PRINT LINER NOTES**

5. *RUGRATS* **THEME WRITTEN BY DEVO**

1. ALL-STAR LINEUP TO "RAP" THE BIBLE

TABLOID This is not yet a "go" project, so hip-hop fans will have to wait for the appearance of a twenty-CD box set with a cast of thousands of their favorite MCs. I vote for Busta Rhymes as Moses and the three wise men to be played by old-schoolers Run-D.M.C.

2. MAGICIAN FAKES OWN CREMATION

TABLOID Harry Houdini, though, vowed to send a message from the grave after his death. Unfortunately, the legendary magician spoke with a heavy accent, and no one understood a word.

3. NEW FOR COUCH POTATOES! ORGANIC TV DINNERS

TRUTH A company called Cascadia Farm distributes frozen organic dinners like Country Herb, which consists of rice, vegetables, and grilled chicken strips with a savory herb sauce. Goes down well with any additive-enhanced cheap beer.

4. GRATEFUL DEAD CD TO FEATURE LARGE PRINT LINER NOTES

TABLOID Fans of the Dead can *see;* they just can't *hear.*

5. *RUGRATS* THEME WRITTEN BY DEVO

TRUTH The theme to the *Rugrats* TV show was written by head Devo Mark Mothersbaugh, who also had a hand in composing the group's unforgettable eighties hit "Jocko Homo." Also, age fifty-plus Mothersbaugh produced an album of music inspired by *The Powerpuff Girls,* another children's cartoon show.

GAME 2

Are the following headlines **TRUTH** *or* **TABLOID?**
(See next page for correct answers.)

1. GARAGE BAND ASPHYXIATED BY CAR FUMES

2. UFO BUFF SINGS TO ATTRACT ALIENS

3. OPERA DIVA SELLS GIRL SCOUT COOKIES

4. AGING DISCO BUFF SHATTERS HIP DOING "THE BUMP"

5. MICROSOFT BILLIONAIRE RECORDS PSYCHEDELIC CD

1. GARAGE BAND ASPHYXIATED BY CAR FUMES

TABLOID However, in 1999, there was a charity event called "Garage Bands for Africa." Which probably was, like, held at Todd's house because his parents were, like, out of town for the weekend.

2. UFO BUFF SINGS TO ATTRACT ALIENS

TABLOID Not quite, but Gyorgy Mandics of Timisoara, Romania, has learned eighteen languages with the hope of improving his chances of communicating with UFO aliens. He's convinced that many words are the same throughout the universe and that knowing multiple languages will increase the possibility of interstellar understanding.

3. OPERA DIVA SELLS GIRL SCOUT COOKIES

TRUTH Internationally renowned opera star Jessye Norman is also an honorary lifetime Girl Scout. During a recent selling season, Norman unloaded two thousand boxes of cookies on her fellow sopranos, contraltos, and tenors, which may explain why the orchestra pit was knee-deep in crumbs.

4. AGING DISCO BUFF SHATTERS HIP DOING "THE BUMP"

TABLOID That's about as likely to happen as John Travolta starring in another sequel to *Saturday Night Fever*.

5. MICROSOFT BILLIONAIRE RECORDS PSYCHEDELIC CD

TRUTH In addition to building his $100-million pop-music museum in Seattle, Paul Allen formed a rock band called Grown Men. The group released a self-titled album featuring Paul on guitar. He also wrote timeless lyrics like "I see you standing there/You call out my name and brush back your hair." According to one reviewer, the "players manage to sculpt a sound reminiscent of an early Pink Floyd album—minus the talent, of course."

GAME 3

Are the following headlines **TRUTH** *or* **TABLOID?**
(See next page for correct answers.)

1. SLAPSTICK COMIC HIT IN FACE BY 14,000 PIES

2. *BOWLING FOR DOLLARS* RATED #1 IN '51

3. MAN WITH WOODEN LEG INVENTS SHOCK-TV TALK

4. TV'S FIRST TALKING CAR WAS A 1931 PACKARD

5. *REAL MCCOYS* GRANDPA HAD BIGGER POP HIT THAN J. LO

1. SLAPSTICK COMIC HIT IN FACE BY 14,000 PIES

TRUTH Old-school TV comic Soupy Sales estimates that he's been hit by more than fourteen thousand pies—including four hundred on one show—during his long and illustrious career. Soupy began his career as host of a Detroit kids' program in the early 1950s. He hit his peak in the mid-1960s, when Hollywood celebrities, including Frank Sinatra, begged to be hit by a pie on Soupy's show.

2. *BOWLING FOR DOLLARS* RATED #1 IN '51

TABLOID Bowling was popular in TV's early days, but *Arthur Godfrey's Talent Scouts* was the number-one show of the fall 1951 season. Arthur Godfrey—who, in my opinion, often appears soused in kinescopes—was as popular as Oprah back then.

3. MAN WITH WOODEN LEG INVENTS SHOCK-TV TALK

TRUTH Joe Pyne had a wooden leg and a syndicated TV talk show in the sixties. His controversial program featured screaming and ranting, plus guests like George Lincoln Rockwell, then head of the American Nazi Party. Many television historians see Joe Pyne as the first step of the long march leading to Jerry Springer and beyond.

4. TV's FIRST TALKING CAR WAS A 1931 PACKARD

TABLOID The real star of *My Mother the Car* was a 1928 Porter, a make-believe model created by the show's writers.

5. *REAL McCOY'S* GRANDPA HAD BIGGER POP HIT THAN J. LO

TABLOID Grizzled Walter Brennan's spoken word "Old Rivers," about a beloved dog, reached number 6 on the Billboard charts in May 1962. J. Lo's "On the 6" hit number 1 a few years ago.

GAME 4

Are the following headlines **TRUTH** *or* **TABLOID?**
(See next page for correct answers.)

1. **Found! 350 Bar Bands Named "Free Beer"**

2. **Being Delusional Helps His Career, Says Will Smith**

3. **Rock 'N' Roll Museum Honors Air Guitar**

4. **Unsung Junkyards Profiled In Lavish Book**

5. **Mayor Asks Ozzfest To "Unplug, Save Energy"**

1. FOUND! 350 BAR BANDS NAMED "FREE BEER"

TABLOID There aren't that many, although cleverly named Free Beer bands are scattered across the country. A comprehensive Internet search found that a Free Beer band recently played these gigs: Polanka Park, in Bensalem, Pennsylvania; X Club, in Denton, Texas, opening for Laughing Stock; and Cotton Patch, in Augusta, Georgia.

2. BEING DELUSIONAL HELPS HIS CAREER, SAYS WILL SMITH

TRUTH When asked how he got to where he is today, the handsome star of *Ali* and *Men in Black* replied, "There's a wonderful delusional quality I possess that allows me to attempt things that are really bad ideas."

3. ROCK 'N' ROLL MUSEUM HONORS AIR GUITAR

TABLOID However, the day may arrive when intense, sweaty men (like me) who strum power chords on invisible guitars to the sound of AC/DC's "Back in Black" are duly recognized. There's an annual Air Guitar World Championship in Oulu, Finland, and a CD entitled *The Best Air Guitar Album in the World . . . Ever*. Why, then, are air guitarists being ignored by the Rock 'n' Roll Museum?

4. UNSUNG JUNKYARDS PROFILED IN LAVISH BOOK

TRUTH The lavishly illustrated *Salvage Yard Treasures of America* is packed with "many never-seen-before photos" of out-of-the-way junkyards, in case you're tired of those usual, done-to-death junkyards.

5. MAYOR ASKS OZZFEST TO "UNPLUG, SAVE ENERGY"

TABLOID The heavy-metal festival headlined by Ozzy Osbourne has toured the United States many times, yet no civic father has dared to ask Ozzfest to turn acoustic in the name of energy conservation.

GAME 5

Are the following headlines **TRUTH** *or* **TABLOID**?
(See next page for correct answers.)

1. TV CRITIC QUITS AFTER VIEWING "HELLISH" FALL SHOWS

2. TEENS SAY "NO WAY" BURT REYNOLDS POSED NUDE

3. EDDIE MURPHY ASKED TO PORTRAY ENTIRE JACKSON FIVE

4. ACCORDIONISTS DEMONSTRATE ON U.S. CAPITOL STEPS

5. DJ NEARLY DECAPITATES FAN WITH FLYING VINYL

And now, for the CORRECT ANSWERS to GAME 5:

1. TV CRITIC QUITS AFTER VIEWING "HELLISH" FALL SHOWS

TABLOID But there can't be a TV critic who doesn't think about quitting at least once a day.

2. TEENS SAY "NO WAY" BURT REYNOLDS POSED NUDE

TABLOID First, most teens don't know who the heck he is. Second, the once wildly popular star of *Smokey and the Bandit* and *Cannonball Run* probably has a hard time believing it, too, because it was way back in 1972 that he was a nude centerfold in *Cosmopolitan* magazine.

3. EDDIE MURPHY ASKED TO PORTRAY ENTIRE JACKSON FIVE

TABLOID If he could play the entire Klump family in both *Nutty Professor* movies, why not Michael, Tito, and the rest? Janet, too.

4. ACCORDIONISTS DEMONSTRATE ON U.S. CAPITOL STEPS

TRUTH A highlight of the American Accordionists Association convention in Washington, D.C., was a mass recital on the steps of the Capitol. Workshops at the convention included "Earning a Living with the Accordion" and "The Accordion in Cyberspace." Rumor has it that strict new security measures are being implemented by Congress to prevent a repeat performance.

5. DJ NEARLY DECAPITATES FAN WITH FLYING VINYL

TABLOID "But if anybody finds my Moby twelve-inch, please return it to the booth."

GAME 6

Are the following headlines **TRUTH *or* TABLOID?**

(See next page for correct answers.)

1. J. Lo's A** Honored With Award

2. Artist Etches Roma Downey On Head Of A Pin

3. Rock 'n' Roller Fathers 33 Kids

4. Rare Sex Book Has 4,000 "Hot" Pages

5. Rap Label Signs Only Felons!

1. J. Lo's A** Honored With Award

TRUTH In a poll of ten thousand people conducted by the British magazine *Celebrity Bodies*, J. Lo was an overwhelming choice for best bottom. In addition, the perfect woman, according to readers, had Catherine Zeta-Jones's face, Posh Spice's legs, Jennifer Aniston's hair, Geri Halliwell's abs, and the bosom of somebody named Kelly Brooks.

2. Artist Etches Roma Downey On Head Of A Pin

TABLOID Seems like the star of *Touched By an Angel* has an ego so big, you couldn't fit her head on a rivet.

3. Rock 'n' Roller Fathers 33 Kids

TRUTH And we're not talking about Mick Jagger. Legendary shouter Screamin' Jay Hawkins made a last request before his death at age seventy: to gather all his children under one roof for the first time. Thirty-three verifiable offspring turned up. By the way, Screamin' was married six times and was known for numerous one-night stands during his extensive touring schedule.

4. Rare Sex Book Has 4,000 "Hot" Pages

TRUTH The autobiographical work *My Secret Life*, by "Walter," was originally published in eleven volumes, a total of four thousand pages in length. Original editions are rare and said to be priceless.

5. Rap Label Signs Only Felons!

TABLOID For now.

Record exec to aspiring rapper: "Sorry, man, rhymes are great, but your rap sheet is a little weak. Jack a car or somethin' and get back to me."

GAME 7

Are the following headlines TRUTH *or* TABLOID?
(See next page for correct answers.)

1. INDIA'S HIGHEST PAID ACTOR IS AN ELEPHANT

2. SCOTLAND IS TOP LOCATION FOR "BOLLYWOOD" FILMS

3. FOUR PEOPLE KILLED WHEN ACTOR SAYS NOTHING

4. GANGSTER-BACKED MOVIE PLAYS TO PACKED HOUSES

5. STARS DON'T WIN "OSCARS" BECAUSE OF THEIR ACTING!

1. INDIA'S HIGHEST PAID ACTOR IS AN ELEPHANT

TABLOID Although many elephants have paraded through "Bollywood" spectacles—the nickname given to Indian movies—none is highly paid. By the way, Bollywood churns out around six hundred movies a year, far more than the Hollywood studios.

2. SCOTLAND IS TOP LOCATION FOR "BOLLYWOOD" FILMS

TRUTH Yes, verdant Scotland is the top location for India's popular movies, which feature beautiful actors, musical numbers, and, seemingly, always a happy ending. Switzerland came in second.

3. FOUR PEOPLE KILLED WHEN ACTOR SAYS NOTHING

TRUTH Four were shot dead when five thousand rioters stormed a Kathmandu movie theater after famed Indian film star Hrithik Roshan was accused of making anti-Nepal slurs, even though a tape of a TV interview revealed he'd said nothing of the sort. Claimed Roshan, "I have never spoken against Nepal or the Nepalese people, whom I love." The theater was playing Roshan's newest film, *Mission Kashmir*.

4. GANGSTER-BACKED MOVIE PLAYS TO PACKED HOUSES

TRUTH *Stealthily, Secretly* played to packed houses in Bombay, even though its producers were alleged gangsters who were already under arrest. The government retained all box-office receipts until the cases against producer Nadeem Rizvi and his financial partner, Bharat Shah, were settled.

5. STARS DON'T WIN "OSCARS" BECAUSE OF THEIR ACTING!

TRUTH Three of sixteen jury members at India's "Oscars" resigned after claiming that winners were chosen based on family ties instead of acting talent. Included among the remaining jury members was the uncle of Raveena Tandon, who received the Best Actress award. Said Ms. Tandon, "I come from a film family and just because I am nominated for an award, I cannot ask my relative to quit the jury."

GAME 8

Are the following headlines **TRUTH** *or* **TABLOID?**

(See next page for correct answers.)

1. **WESLEY SNIPES WAS NO MONK**

2. **MONSTER TRUCKS RUNNING OUT OF CARS TO CRUSH**

3. **FEMALE BREAK DANCER MUST WEAR CHADOR**

4. **"BEVERLY HILLBILLIES" BIBLE STUDY GROUPS GROW**

5. **$75,000 TURNTABLE GIVES LPs ROYAL TREATMENT**

And now, for the CORRECT ANSWERS to GAME 8:

1. WESLEY SNIPES WAS NO MONK

TABLOID Wesley claims that he once was a monk, although not the kind with a hood and glowing eyes ripped from the cover of an Iron Maiden CD. In a shocking interview, Wesley revealed that he'd been a "monk" in the romance department because he hadn't had a girlfriend in a while. But take comfort, ladies; Wesley added, "I think this stage is going to end real soon."

2. MONSTER TRUCKS RUNNING OUT OF CARS TO CRUSH

TRUTH In a perhaps fatal blow to the art form, monster-truck shows are quickly depleting the supply of big 1970s gas guzzlers, like Chrysler New Yorkers and LeBarons, that offer more steel and glass to destroy. As Howard Sofield, a veteran monster-truck show manager, says, "We definitely like the full-size cars . . . but they're getting harder to find."

3. FEMALE BREAK DANCER MUST WEAR CHADOR

TABLOID There are no known chador-wearing break dancers, even on MTV Lebanon, based in the city formerly known as war-torn Beirut.

4. "BEVERLY HILLBILLIES" BIBLE STUDY GROUPS GROW

TRUTH In a bid to get more people to study the Bible, some churches have integrated old TV shows into their classes. A company named The Entertainment Ministry sells *The Beverly Hillbillies Bible Study* guide to groups across the United States. Says a company spokesman, "The hillbillies are simple people in a world obsessed by money, but they never let it change them."

5. $75,000 TURNTABLE GIVES LPs ROYAL TREATMENT

TRUTH Yes, new turntables are in production—and not just for dance-club DJs. Although improvements frequently turn up, the premier turntable has been the $75,000 Rockport System III Sirius. Each handmade unit takes about six months to build.

GAME 9

Are the following headlines **TRUTH** *or* **TABLOID**?
(See next page for correct answers.)

1. ELTON JOHN TOPS FUNERAL HOME POP CHARTS

2. FIRST NUDE CALENDAR WAS BY TOULOUSE-LAUTREC

3. CRITIC FLIPS COIN TO DECIDE IF HE "LIKES" MOVIE

4. ELVIS IMPERSONATOR WEARS TURBAN, GROWS BEARD

5. RAPPER "YOUNG M.C." IS NOW MIDDLE-AGED D.A.

1. Elton John Tops Funeral Home Pop Charts

TRUTH According to Kelly Smith of the National Funeral Directors Association, Elton is the most frequently played pop star during funeral proceedings, with Celine Dion placing second. Bach and Beethoven are the top classical artists.

2. First Nude Calendar Was By Toulouse-Lautrec

TABLOID Actually, the first-known calendar nude was a reproduction of a famous painting by fellow Frenchman Paul Chabas. *September Morn* tastefully depicts a nude woman bathing on the edge of a lake and was first published as a calendar in New York in 1913. An outraged member of the Society for the Suppression of Vice unsuccessfully tried to get it banned.

3. Critic Flips Coin To Decide If He "Likes" Movie

TABLOID But do you really think Roger Ebert and his ilk watch four or five crappy movies each week *all the way through*?

4. Elvis Impersonator Wears Turban, Grows Beard

TRUTH In fact, Peter Narawander Singh, a Sikh who resides in Swansea, Wales, does one of the best Elvis tributes around, says party planner Danielle Nay of London. Singh's bearded, turban-wearing, white-sequined–suited Elvis is in such demand that even Bob Geldof wanted him at his fiftieth birthday bash.

5. Rapper "Young M.C." Is Now Middle-Aged D.A.

TABLOID Marvin Young, a.k.a. "Young M.C.," has not given up trying to duplicate the success of his Grammy-winning 1989 rap hit "Bust a Move" to become a hard-hitting district attorney. A University of Southern California graduate with a degree in economics, Young M.C. recorded the little-heard CDs *Return of the 1 Hit Wonder* in 1997 and *Ain't Goin' Out Like That* in 2000 and probably has another comeback in the works.

GAME 10

Are the following headlines **TRUTH** *or* **TABLOID?**
(See next page for correct answers.)

1. CANNED GODZILLA MEAT INVADES JAPAN

2. EZ LISTENING HALL OF FAME OPENS IN AKRON

3. TV CAUSED EARTHQUAKE, SAYS HIGHLY PLACED ZEALOT

4. WINNING LOTTERY NUMBERS PUBLISHED DAY BEFORE DRAWING

5. DESTITUTE MOVIEGOER BEGS FOR POPCORN

1. Canned Godzilla Meat Invades Japan

TRUTH The Japanese have taken the ultimate revenge on the fire-breathing monster by turning him into—canned food. Actually, Godzilla Meat is three and a half ounces of corned beef packed in a tin emblazoned with Godzilla photos. The delicious treat is brought to your tastebuds by toy maker Takara Co., which also created Rodan Meat, a canned barbecue-chicken product named after the flying movie monster.

2. EZ Listening Hall Of Fame Opens In Akron

TABLOID Who would cut the ribbon, John Tesh or Kenny G?

3. TV Caused Earthquake, Says Highly Placed Zealot

TRUTH Ultraconservative cleric Mufti Imtiaz says that immoral TV caused the death of thousands in a killer earthquake that shook India in 2000. In response, followers of the cleric threw hundreds of televisions off rooftops or burned them in bonfires throughout a region about six hundred miles southwest of New Delhi.

4. Winning Lottery Numbers Published Day Before Drawing

TRUTH Weird, but here's how it happened: The computer system crashed at *The Columbian,* an Oregon newspaper. In an attempt to re-create lost material, a copy editor mistakenly printed the winning Pick Four numbers from the Virginia lottery. In a million-to-one coincidence, the *same* winning numbers, 6–8–5–5, were selected the following day in the Oregon lottery. A detective with the Oregon State Police confirmed that no hanky-panky was involved.

5. Destitute Moviegoer Begs For Popcorn

TRUTH People waiting in the concession line at a northwestern movie theater were badgered for change by a fellow moviegoer—who claimed she didn't have enough cash for popcorn. She'd no doubt already spent the rent money on Milk Duds.

SPORTS

It's hard to believe the big money that athletes are paid to hit, bounce, throw, carry, kick, punt, whack, smash, toss, drive, putt, lob, shoot, pass, knock out, lasso, and dunk. It's almost as hard to imagine that beach volleyball and skateboarding are now professional sports and that you can win an Olympic gold medal by riding face first downhill on a skeleton. In fact, there's so much upheaval in the wide world of sports, you'll have a real workout just trying to separate truth from tabloid in these headlines.

GAME 1

Are the following headlines **TRUTH or TABLOID?**
(See next page for correct answers.)

1. SACK RACE HIGHLIGHTS NUDE OLYMPICS

2. OFF-ROAD GOLF CART GIVES NEW HOPE TO HOOKERS

3. AFRICAN SCIENTISTS PROMOTE TUG-OF-WAR RESEARCH

4. TINY FAMILY SITS ATOP DWARF SPORTS WORLD

5. 7TH-INNING SEX REPLACES 7TH-INNING STRETCH

1. SACK RACE HIGHLIGHTS NUDE OLYMPICS

TRUTH At a recent Nude Olympics held in Adelaide, Australia, the lead events were sack racing and three-legged racing. "It's a kind of nudist expo," the games' organizer said. No mention why volleyball—the sport that launched a thousand nudie movies—didn't make the cut.

2. OFF-ROAD GOLF CART GIVES NEW HOPE TO HOOKERS

TRUTH Hookers, slicers, and other bad golfers whose wild swings cause them to take frequent trips into the rough may benefit from this trend— the conversion of golf carts into off-road vehicles. First used by farmers and hunters, the converted carts feature knobby tires, increased stability, and sometimes even camouflage paint.

3. AFRICAN SCIENTISTS PROMOTE TUG-OF-WAR RESEARCH

TRUTH Tug-of-war may have been canceled as an Olympic event in the early twentieth century, but don't tell the sport's millions of dedicated players around the world that it's not serious business. Organized competitions take place from Scotland to Japan, but in South Africa, science is being applied to the game. Researchers at the University of Pretoria have investigated the biomechanics of tug-of-war in order to improve the performance of players.

4. TINY FAMILY SITS ATOP DWARF SPORTS WORLD

TRUTH Peter and Liz Holland, along with their two children, won an amazing eleven medals at the World Dwarf Games in Canada. The Leeds, England, clan dominated events ranging from sprints to swimming, shot put, discus, and javelin. Approximately 350 athletes took part, none of whom was taller than four feet ten inches.

5. 7TH-INNING SEX REPLACES 7TH-INNING STRETCH

TABLOID The cheap seats haven't gotten that cheap yet.

GAME 2

Are the following headlines **TRUTH** *or* **TABLOID**?
(See next page for correct answers.)

1. AMERICA'S FIRST EXTREME SPORT WAS EYE-GOUGING

2. IT WAS ONCE IMPOSSIBLE TO WEAR A BASEBALL HAT
   BACKWARD

3. BASEBALL SKEPTICS CLAIM CURVE IS OPTICAL ILLUSION

4. 1921: AMERICA'S #1 PRO WRESTLER IS POLISH INTELLECTUAL

5. NYC COPS ORDERED TO BREAK KIDS' SLEDS TO BITS

1. AMERICA'S FIRST EXTREME SPORT WAS EYE-GOUGING

TRUTH Around 1800, there was nothing an extreme sports fan liked better than to sit on the grass, sip on a grog, and watch a hard-fought "gouging" match. The sport was wrestling with a twist. The chief goal was to pop out your opponent's eye with your thumb. "Gougers" grew long thumbnails for an added advantage. The upside? You couldn't lose more than twice.

2. IT WAS ONCE IMPOSSIBLE TO WEAR A BASEBALL HAT BACKWARD

TRUTH That's because the players wore stylish straw boaters with perfectly round brims. The nineteenth-century uniform also included white shirts and blue trousers. Imagine Mark McGwire dressed like Fred Astaire and you get the picture.

3. BASEBALL SKEPTICS CLAIM CURVE IS OPTICAL ILLUSION

TRUTH In the early days of the curveball, many observers believed that it was a trick played on the mind. The observers, undoubtedly, were umpires.

4. 1921: AMERICA'S #1 PRO WRESTLER IS POLISH INTELLECTUAL

TRUTH Stanislaus Zbyszko didn't have a name as catchy as Stone Cold Steve Austin, but he was a great wrestler back in the day. Born in Poland, Stanislaus spoke twelve languages, earned a law degree from the University of Vienna, and was a classical pianist. But his greatest claim to fame was beating Strangler Lewis for the title in 1921. History does not tell us whether Stanislaus choked Strangler with a piano wire or pounded him mercilessly with his law degree. Note: Stanislaus's real last name was Cyganiewicz, which apparently didn't roll off the tongue like Zbyszko.

5. NYC COPS ORDERED TO BREAK KIDS' SLEDS TO BITS

TRUTH Looks like back in 1713, kids on sleds were as irritating as skateboarders are today. The powers-that-be told New York cops to take any sled in the possession of a child "within ye said city" and "breake" it into bits.

GAME 3

Are the following headlines **TRUTH *or* TABLOID?**
(See next page for correct answers.)

1. **Pro Golfer Pretends Ball Is Her Hubby**

2. **Sports Shrink: "To Win, Play To Lose"**

3. **Pit Crew Refuses To Put Air In Jeff Gordon's Tires**

4. **Fan Collects Broken Hockey Player Teeth**

5. **Purist Anglers Catch Fish With Their Hands**

1. PRO GOLFER PRETENDS BALL IS HER HUBBY

TABLOID But there are about as many ways to prepare for the mental side of golf as there are players. In fact, a recent count found 115 books devoted to the subject, not to mention countless articles and videotapes. So how come most of us still can't break 90?

2. SPORTS SHRINK: "TO WIN, PLAY TO LOSE"

TABLOID Unfortunately, most sports psychology books are along the lines of *How to Win at Sport and Life through Mental Cruelty* and *F*****g with Your Opponent's Head*.

3. PIT CREW REFUSES TO PUT AIR IN JEFF GORDON'S TIRES

TRUTH In the competitive world of auto racing, plain ol' air isn't good enough anymore. In order to minimize the performance-altering expansion of a tire during a race, a pit crew will inflate it with nitrogen, which remains more stable when heated.

4. FAN COLLECTS BROKEN HOCKEY PLAYER TEETH

TABLOID I haven't seen any busted incisors offered for auction on-line, even though many have been shattered in the course of the game. But "puck teeth" are one of the most popular joke dentures sold by novelty stores, along with "*Deliverance* teeth," snaggle teeth, and, of course, Austin Powers choppers.

5. PURIST ANGLERS CATCH FISH WITH THEIR HANDS

TRUTH Real fishermen "noodle." That's what the technique of fishing by hand, primarily for catfish, is called. Wanna try? Here's how: Stick your hand in the water. Wiggle fingers. When fish bites, thrust arm down its throat until it stops fighting. Then fry in pan with salt and pepper, remembering to remove arm first.

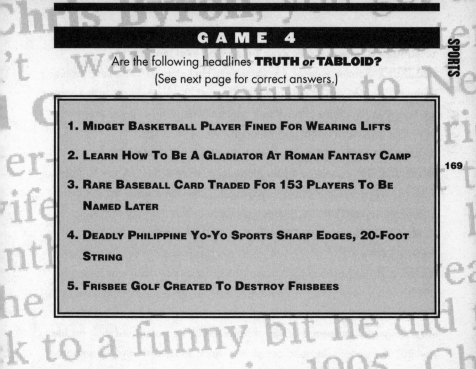

GAME 4

Are the following headlines **TRUTH *or* TABLOID?**

(See next page for correct answers.)

1. **MIDGET BASKETBALL PLAYER FINED FOR WEARING LIFTS**

2. **LEARN HOW TO BE A GLADIATOR AT ROMAN FANTASY CAMP**

3. **RARE BASEBALL CARD TRADED FOR 153 PLAYERS TO BE NAMED LATER**

4. **DEADLY PHILIPPINE YO-YO SPORTS SHARP EDGES, 20-FOOT STRING**

5. **FRISBEE GOLF CREATED TO DESTROY FRISBEES**

1. Midget Basketball Player Fined For Wearing Lifts

TABLOID Farmer Pete of the Canadian Half-pints, a successful professional midget basketball team, claims, "You can't disqualify me from shooting hoops just because of my size. I can shoot as well as any average-size man. Our approach is that people laugh with us, not at us."

2. Learn How To Be A Gladiator At Roman Fantasy Camp

TRUTH You can live out your gladiator fantasy at the Sculoa Gladiatori in Rome. A hundred bucks allows you to do battle with spears, axes, tridents, and thirteen-pound shields. Unfortunately, you must bring your own tunic.

3. Rare Baseball Card Traded For 153 Players To Be Named Later

TABLOID The baseball-card game isn't as loony now as it was during the 1980s, when some hobbyists tried to turn it into a big business, buying and selling cards by the crate load. In one case, a trader filled his dining room to the ceiling with unopened boxes of Topps cards he purchased with his life savings. The bottom dropped out of the market soon afterward, so the only one to make a killing was probably his wife.

4. Deadly Philippine Yo-Yo Sports Sharp Edges, 20-Foot String

TRUTH Yo-yo means "come back" in Tagalog, the native Filipino tongue. It was originally a weapon, with sharp edges and studs, attached to a twenty-foot rope for flinging at enemies or prey.

Cop: "Drop that yo-yo and walk backward toward me!"

Perpetrator: "You'll have to pry it from my cold, dead hands!"

5. Frisbee Golf Created To Destroy Frisbees

TRUTH "Steady" Ed Headrick left a secure job as vice president of a water-heater manufacturer to work for Wham-O in 1964. In 1975, he devised Frisbee, or Disc Golf, which he perhaps jokingly claimed would be "a game where people would throw an expensive Frisbee into the ground every throw on purpose. Wow! What a market potential." Today two million souls play Frisbee golf, including ten thousand professionals—who hopefully have kept their day jobs.

GAME 5

Are the following headlines **TRUTH** *or* **TABLOID**?
(See next page for correct answers.)

1. ATTACK HELICOPTER STRAFES PLAYING FIELD WITH
   PAINTBALLS

2. "TOTAL PAINTBALL" PLAYERS LOAD GUNS WITH TOXIC PAINT

3. GREEN BAY PACKERS BOND OVER PAINTBALL

4. PAINTBALLERS OBTAIN WEAPONS OF MASS DESTRUCTION!

5. "PAINTBALL NAPALM" SCALDS PLAYERS WITH HOT,
   GOOEY PAINT

171

1. ATTACK HELICOPTER STRAFES PLAYING FIELD WITH PAINTBALLS

TRUTH Helicopters ranging from Bell two-seaters to Vietnam-era Hueys are an increasingly common sight at large-scale paintball events. "Death from above" is rained down on players via automatic guns. As one terrified foot soldier says, "The only defense is found beneath a big tree or thick bush."

2. "TOTAL PAINTBALL" PLAYERS LOAD GUNS WITH TOXIC PAINT

TABLOID Today's paintball players are environmentally conscious fighting men. But the first paint used in the early eighties was indelible, toxic, and nonbiodegradable. Thirty-five million dollars in lawsuits forced the manufacturer to change.

3. GREEN BAY PACKERS BOND OVER PAINTBALL

TRUTH "It breaks the ice," claims one Packer. "A lot of people don't know much about one another, but by going out and doing things like this, you can always go back to that paintball game and start joking and create a conversation." Aww . . . isn't that sweet.

4. PAINTBALLERS OBTAIN WEAPONS OF MASS DESTRUCTION!

TRUTH Not many people know paintball has such terrible weapons, but here's a sampling: 1. Paint grenades are thrown by hand or shot from a launcher and cost anywhere from five to twenty-five dollars each; 2. When an unsuspecting player triggers a paintball land mine, the contents are sprayed over a fifteen-foot-diameter "killing zone"; 3. The paint mortar has a range of more than 250 feet. "This baby cooks!" an ad for it proclaims.

5. "PAINTBALL NAPALM" SCALDS PLAYERS WITH HOT, GOOEY PAINT

TABLOID The paintball envelope hasn't been pushed that far yet. The closest to it at this point is a so-called water balloon paint bomb that's dropped from a helicopter or an airplane.

GAME 6

Are the following headlines **TRUTH** *or* **TABLOID?**

(See next page for correct answers.)

1. RACE FANS COLLECT EXHAUST FUMES OF FAVORITE CARS

2. NASCAR COMIC BOOK REQUIRED FOR WRITERS

3. RACE FANS COLLECT FLAT TIRES OF FAVORITE DRIVERS

4. HARRIED NASCAR PIT CREW SERVICES WRONG CAR

5. BULLETPROOF HELMET PROTECTS RACER'S SWELLED HEAD

And now, for the CORRECT ANSWERS to GAME 6:

1. RACE FANS COLLECT EXHAUST FUMES OF FAVORITE CARS

TRUTH Ferrari fans are a rabid lot, collecting anything to do with the exotic car, even when they can't afford the actual vehicle. Recently, fumes from a Ferrari race car were collected, bottled, and sold for about four hundred dollars.

2. NASCAR COMIC BOOK REQUIRED FOR WRITERS

TRUTH If you're a student in Ms. Petty's eighth-grade creative writing class at Shallotte Middle School in North Carolina, *Race Warrior* is an essential text. The comic book about stock-car racing in the future helps students learn about characterization, plot, and dialogue, says Ms. Petty. Not to mention how to send Dale Jarrett into the wall.

3. RACE FANS COLLECT FLAT TIRES OF FAVORITE DRIVERS

TRUTH Flat tires belonging to NASCAR race stars are often sold at events. Fans have been known to turn a Rusty Wallace right rear into a glass-topped coffee table and a Bobby LaBonte rain tire into a wall-hanging that's sure to start a conversation.

4. HARRIED NASCAR PIT CREW SERVICES WRONG CAR

TABLOID Even though two or three dozen cars may enter the pits simultaneously, no NASCAR pit crew has made this mistake. However, more than a few lug nuts have been forgotten, causing wheels to wobble or fall off at speeds up to 200 mph.

5. BULLETPROOF HELMET PROTECTS RACER'S SWELLED HEAD

TRUTH A helmet belonging Formula One legend Michael Schumacher was made of bulletproof Kevlar and other materials. Sources at Ferrari said the extremely self-assured driver—paid in the range of thirty million dollars a year—was unlikely to be the target of a bullet. But, hey, anything for a little publicity.

GAME 7

Are the following headlines **TRUTH** *or* **TABLOID**?
(See next page for correct answers.)

---

1. **GOLFER DISQUALIFIED FOR BEING HONEST**

2. **OBSESSIVE/COMPULSIVE ATHLETE ENTERS SPECIAL OLYMPICS**

3. **TRENDY BOWLERS PLAGUE ALLEYS, STEAL SHOES**

4. **HIGH SEAS HAMPER CRUISE SHIP MARATHON RUN**

5. **FIRESTONE INKS "WIN-WIN-WIN-WIN" AGREEMENT**

---

1. GOLFER DISQUALIFIED FOR BEING HONEST

TRUTH Actually, pro golfer Greg Chalmers cost himself nearly one hundred thousand dollars by being honest twice. First, Chalmers told a competitor's caddie that he hit a six iron after a bad tee shot at a Kemper Open. It's a technical violation of the PGA rule that golfers can't give each other advice during a round. Two days later, when Chalmers learned that he'd broken the rule, he told the rules committee, which had been unaware of the incident. The result? Chalmers was disqualified from the tournament, losing the prize money.

2. OBSESSIVE/COMPULSIVE ATHLETE ENTERS SPECIAL OLYMPICS

TABLOID Unfortunately, the Special Olympics does not cater to OCD sufferers, although I've written 33,529 letters pleading with them to include such events.

3. TRENDY BOWLERS PLAGUE ALLEYS, STEAL SHOES

TRUTH Weren't bowling shoes a fashion fad back in the eighties? Well, they are again, in some places. Many bowling alleys added laser lights and loud music to attract a younger crowd. They succeeded, but the new bowlers are swiping the rental shoes right and left. One bowling alley near Boston says it loses about 150 pairs of shoes annually.

4. HIGH SEAS HAMPER CRUISE SHIP MARATHON RUN

TRUTH The good ship *Lyubov Orlova* was scheduled to drop a group of wealthy running fanatics off in Antarctica to take part in a marathon. But when gale-velocity winds prevented a landing, the 108 passengers decided to stage the event onboard. It took 422 laps around the deck to complete the 26.2 mile run, with participants sustaining many minor injuries due to the rough seas. Price tag for the ten-day tour: $4,000 to $5,500.

5. FIRESTONE INKS "WIN-WIN-WIN-WIN" AGREEMENT

TRUTH Today's creative reworking of a cliché goes to the Bridgestone/Firestone spokesman who said the following about a race to be held at the Texas Motor Speedway: "This sponsorship connects us with a world-class racing facility and a great competition where our tires will be an integral part of the excitement. It's really a win-win-win-win relationship for Firestone, the speedway, the series, and the fans."

GAME 8

Are the following headlines **TRUTH** *or* **TABLOID?**
(See next page for correct answers.)

1. **U**MPIRE **F**ILLS **G**ARAGE **W**ITH **S**TOLEN **B**ASEBALLS

2. **A**CTIVISTS **D**EMAND **G**REEN **B**AY **P**ACKERS **C**HANGE **N**AME

3. **7-Y**EAR-**O**LD **B**OY **S**AVES **M**OUNTAIN **C**LIMBERS **F**ROM **D**EATH

4. **D**AD **B**RIBES **U**MP **T**O "**F**IX" **5-Y**EAR-**O**LD'S **T-B**ALL **G**AME

5. **R**UTGERS **M**INIATURE **G**OLF **C**OURSE **L**URES **N**EW **S**TUDENTS

1. UMPIRE FILLS GARAGE WITH STOLEN BASEBALLS

TABLOID Come to think of it, what really happens to the balls that umpires hide behind their chest protectors?

2. ACTIVISTS DEMAND GREEN BAY PACKERS CHANGE NAME

TRUTH People for the Ethical Treatment of Animals (PETA) recently asked the Green Bay Packers football team to change its name. PETA claimed the name promotes violence and bloodshed because it refers to meat packers, or those who work in slaughterhouses. They insisted the team's name be changed to "Six-Packers" or "Pickers," as in fruit pickers. A spokesman for the eighty-one-year-old team says no change is likely. To annoy activists even more, how about these suggestions: Green Bay Tripe, Green Bay Gutslingers, Green Bay Headcheese?

3. 7-YEAR-OLD BOY SAVES MOUNTAIN CLIMBERS FROM DEATH

TRUTH Fletcher Wood, seven, was playing in his backyard with his toy walkie-talkie when he heard strange voices asking for help. The men said they were mountain climbers who'd been injured in a rock slide on 11,240-foot Mount Hood in Oregon. Fletcher was an incredible eighty-one miles away in the small town of McMinnville. The level-headed kid alerted his dad, who called the police. A rescue squad was sent by helicopter and saved the two astonished climbers.

4. DAD BRIBES UMP TO "FIX" 5-YEAR-OLD'S T-BALL GAME

TABLOID Dad to ump: "If we win, I'll take you to Pizza Hut with us after the game!"

5. RUTGERS MINIATURE GOLF COURSE LURES NEW STUDENTS

TRUTH Rutgers students can now play miniature golf on their very own course. This is just part of a nationwide multibillion-dollar effort on the part of universities to make their campuses more attractive to those students whose well-off families can afford full tuition. Bonus: Any student who aces the eighteenth hole wins a lap dance from a full professor.

GAME 9

Are the following headlines **TRUTH** *or* **TABLOID?**
(See next page for correct answers.)

179

1. **HOT-HEADED TENNIS PRO WRECKS RACQUETS, LOSES MATCH**

2. **ESPN DECLARES RAP METAL AN EXTREME SPORT**

3. **MARATHON RUNNER BLAMES FISH AND CHIPS ON DEFEAT**

4. **RICH HIPPIE LAUNCHES PRO HACKY-SACK LEAGUE**

5. **"TIGER WOODS OF MINIATURE GOLF" WINS 23RD TOURNEY**

1. HOT-HEADED TENNIS PRO WRECKS RACQUETS, LOSES MATCH

TRUTH Goren Ivanisevic wasn't happy with his game at the Samsung Open in England. So he smashed his racquets until all three lay twisted and broken. Lacking anything with which to continue play, he was forced to abandon the match. Luckily, he wasn't playing handball.

2. ESPN DECLARES RAP METAL AN EXTREME SPORT

TABLOID Although listening to an entire Limp Bizkit CD is a true test of courage.

3. MARATHON RUNNER BLAMES FISH AND CHIPS ON DEFEAT

TABLOID Common sense, though, indicates it's not a good idea to consume greasy food before running twenty-six miles. However, I once knew a guy who drank Guinness from paper cups provided by friends stationed along the course. He detoured to find a rest room and finished 18,293rd, but didn't much care.

4. RICH HIPPIE LAUNCHES PRO HACKY-SACK LEAGUE

TABLOID What some damn hippie has done is invented a type of hacky-sack where you kick the "footbag" over a badminton net. In case you're interested, here's important advice from a prominent footbag website: "For playing Footbag Net, the choice of footbag is very important. . . . Look for round, firm, and sturdy footbags, i.e., footbags that don't break in too much, hold their shape, and aren't too hard to kick straight up or over the net. The Net Juice by Flying Clipper Footbags is the current bag of choice by most advanced footbag net players."

5. "TIGER WOODS OF MINIATURE GOLF" WINS 23RD TOURNEY

TABLOID While there will no doubt one day appear a hero who'll return miniature golf to its rightful place atop the sports world, he or she has yet to putt the ball through the clown's mouth, so to speak.

GAME 10

Are the following headlines **TRUTH** *or* **TABLOID?**
(See next page for correct answers.)

1. PRIZE COW DRAPED WITH BULLETPROOF BLANKET IN HUNTING SEASON

2. MORE AND MORE COLLEGES OFFER GOLF AS A MAJOR

3. "MILLION KID TUG-OF-WAR" PLANNED ON WASHINGTON MALL

4. FARMERS CHOP CROPS WITH MARTIAL ARTS WEAPONS

5. DISC GOLF CHANGES LIVES OF TROUBLED STUDENTS

1. PRIZE COW DRAPED WITH BULLETPROOF BLANKET IN HUNTING SEASON

TABLOID Every deer-hunting season, a few cows, horses, and even humans are mistakenly fired upon, so maybe bulletproof protection should be the order of the day for anyone venturing into the sport's "kill zone."

2. MORE AND MORE COLLEGES OFFER GOLF AS A MAJOR

TRUTH Eight United States universities offer golf as a major, up from four schools a couple of years ago. In other words, you can now actually graduate with a degree in golf. More than fourteen hundred students are currently enrolled in the "grueling" curriculum, as many undergrads describe it. The Methodist College website claims its program allows you to "build your game as you build your academic and professional career."

3. "MILLION KID TUG-OF-WAR" PLANNED ON WASHINGTON MALL

TABLOID What a glorious climax to summer camp it could one day provide this nation's youngsters! Other camp-related events might include the Mosquito Bite Count, Three-Legged Race for One-Legged Kids, Cookie Toss, and Sunburned Skin Peel-off.

4. FARMERS CHOP CROPS WITH MARTIAL ARTS WEAPONS

TRUTH Remember the nunchaku—the martial arts weapon that Bruce Lee whipped around in his movies? The two sticks connected by a chain? Well, the nunchaku was used by farmers in Okinawa to flail rice and other crops before they found it was also good for whipping a**.

5. DISC GOLF CHANGES LIVES OF TROUBLED STUDENTS

TRUTH At least that's what Ed Headrick, inventor of Disc Golf, says. On a Web site, he claims, "Yes, Disc Golf is an academic resource, it teaches an amazing peace of mind to students who have never been taught to deal on a one-on-one basis with themselves. In Disc Golf, troubled students learn to participate in an activity that indeed changes their lives." Putting his money where his mouth is, Mr. Headrick offers 25 percent off the price of a "complete Disc Golf course" to institutions, including military bases, mental hospitals, and correctional facilities for young people.

CHAPTER 10

SCIENCE *AND* NATURE

Through the years researchers have conducted many dubious investigations, like whether seeing ghosts is the result of brain damage and which wild animals prefer to defecate in the same pile. In addition, scientific research has resulted in many wonders for use in our daily lives, from the toaster oven to the glow-in-the-dark condom and the snazzy Velcro wallet. But one thing scientists have never designed is a foolproof bull**** detector—which you might find handy in this section.

GAME 1

Are the following headlines **TRUTH *or* TABLOID?**
(See next page for correct answers.)

1. FRENCH-KISSING NEARLY AS EFFECTIVE AS CPR

2. MORE HUSBANDS STRAY THAN DOGS

3. SCIENTISTS BREED STONED MICE THAT DON'T GET THE MUNCHIES

4. NOW TRANSSEXUAL WANTS TO CHANGE SPECIES, TOO!

5. IDENTICAL TWINS GIVE BIRTH TO IDENTICAL TWINS

1. French-Kissing Nearly As Effective As CPR

TRUTH Surprisingly, neither activity is much help when performed by an amateur. A fascinating survey of nearly 300 people published in *Academic Emergency Medicine* found that 96 percent believed that CPR was effective a whopping two-thirds of the time. But, in real life, CPR rarely works. A New York study of 2,329 cases of cardiac arrest found that just 3 percent of victims who received CPR from bystanders survived. In other words, almost everyone who receives CPR from a nonprofessional dies, so CPR performed by an amateur will no more save a life than a French kiss will.

2. More Husbands Stray Than Dogs

TABLOID This is another one of those questions that deserves a great deal more study. Perhaps a crack team of social scientists, angry wives, and dogcatchers will one day provide us with an answer.

3. Scientists Breed Stoned Mice That Don't Get The Munchies

TRUTH Do those scientists ever stop messing around? Here's what they did to some innocent mice: An unsuspecting group of the rodents was genetically engineered to lack the brain receptors for the cannabinoid molecules found in marijuana. The scientists then used a bong (or something) to get the mice fried out of their minds. But the creatures didn't develop an insatiable craving for Velveeta, or whatever they like to munch on while watching their nonstoned buddies run in place on that wheel-thingy. Investigators concluded that cannabinoids are one of two key chemicals that control hunger in the brain.

4. Now Transsexual Wants To Change Species, Too!

TABLOID "From the age of five, Sven knew he didn't fit in with the other boys and their silly games. Deep inside there was a Siberian musk ox dying to get out and gore a nomad. Yes, he needed a transspecies operation. But how to tell dear Momma and Poppa?"

5. Identical Twins Give Birth To Identical Twins

TABLOID An unofficial analysis of current cloning trends indicates that in the future, everyone will be identical in appearance, taking the uncertainty out of blind dates, personals ads, and police manhunts.

GAME 2

Are the following headlines **TRUTH** *or* **TABLOID**?
(See next page for correct answers.)

1. **BENEVOLENT WASPS RESCUE WOUNDED TOMATO**

2. **EVERY WILD RHINO DEFECATES IN SAME PILE**

3. **SWISHY FISH "DRESSES IN DRAG"**

4. **VIAGRA HELPS HOUSEPLANTS STAY ERECT**

5. **JANE GOODALL: CHIMPS CAN COMMUNICATE BY
   "RELEASING AIR"**

And now, for the CORRECT ANSWERS to GAME 2:

TRUTH or TABLOID? *(vertical side text)*

1. BENEVOLENT WASPS RESCUE WOUNDED TOMATO

TRUTH As reported in the journal *Nature,* a tomato wounded by army-worms reacted by increasing production of the chemicals responsible for its leafy green odor. The release attracted hungry wasps, who rescued the tomato by eating the militant armyworms. Can an insect win the Nobel Peace Prize?

2. EVERY WILD RHINO DEFECATES IN SAME PILE

TRUTH Rhinos, like most wild animals, identify territorial boundaries with urine and dung. The male rhino hoses the savannah with an incredible twelve-foot stream of urine, and all rhinos in a herd defecate in the same pile. Each rhino then scrapes through the odorous heap with its hind feet in order to spread the scent far and wide, according to observant-beyond-the-call-of-duty researcher Janine Benyus, author of *Beastly Behaviors.*

3. SWISHY FISH "DRESSES IN DRAG"

TRUTH The male giant cuttlefish of Australia is an unrepentant cross-dresser, but not for the reason you may think. A smaller male often tags along with a breeding pair in the guise of a female, adopting the female cuttlefish body color and pattern and withdrawing his webbed "arms." When the dominant male isn't looking, the smaller male mates with his unattended lady friend. Then the interloper once again dons his female disguise and swims safely away from the unsuspecting male fish.

4. VIAGRA HELPS HOUSEPLANTS STAY ERECT

TRUTH Personally, I found this hard to believe. However, researchers at Bar-Llan University in Israel say that a few drops of Viagra in water helps to double the lifespan of plants, while keeping them erect longer. Unfortunately, the high cost of the drug will keep it from the hands of most gardeners.

5. JANE GOODALL: CHIMPS CAN COMMUNICATE BY "RELEASING AIR"

TABLOID Forty years of hiding behind ferns and that's her blockbuster discovery?

GAME 3

Are the following headlines **TRUTH** *or* **TABLOID?**
(See next page for correct answers.)

1. **RETIRED COMBAT DOLPHINS ASSIST TROUBLED CHILDREN**

2. **MEN WITH THICK BODY HAIR ARE USUALLY FAT AND BALD**

3. **CAVEMEN INVENTED DENTAL FLOSS**

4. **JELLYFISH LOVE EXPENSIVE CAVIAR**

5. **COMPUTER CHIP OBSCURES VOICES IN HEAD WITH WHITE NOISE**

1. Retired Combat Dolphins Assist Troubled Children

TRUTH When the Cold War ended, the Ukrainian military had about seventy out-of-work dolphins on its hands. The highly intelligent creatures had been trained at great expense to perform secret underwater tasks. Now many of the dolphins have been retrained to treat children suffering from a variety of illnesses. The chief of the Ukrainian program says that more than two thousand troubled kids have benefited from the psychotherapeutic effects of exposure to the dolphins and their sonar clicks.

2. Men With Thick Body Hair Are Usually Fat And Bald

TABLOID I admit I have no solid evidence to back up this theory. However, I believe it anyway thanks to an eye-opening visit to a health-club steam room with my Uncle Morty and his pals.

3. Cavemen Invented Dental Floss

TABLOID However, anthropologists in Tanzania have discovered signs of toothpick use at a site where human remains dating back as far as 1.8 million years have been unearthed. The researchers say toothpicks became common about the same time early man began eating meat. The tool consisted of bone or grit attached to a stick. Of course, it took another 1.799 million years or so to add mint flavoring.

4. Jellyfish Love Expensive Caviar

TRUTH Some of the world's best caviar comes from Iran. But sturgeon-devouring jellyfish have invaded the waters of the Caspian Sea, causing caviar production to plunge, which makes the sturgeon eggs that the jellyfish are feeding on even more valuable.

5. Computer Chip Obscures Voices In Head With White Noise

TABLOID An early model played *Frampton Comes Alive* but was rejected as too commercial.

GAME 4

Are the following headlines **TRUTH** *or* **TABLOID**?
(See next page for correct answers.)

1. **Ghosts Are The Result Of Brain Damage, Says Scientist**

2. **Viagra Key To Saving Panda From Extinction**

3. **You Can Turn Invisible Spontaneously**

4. **Afterlife Expert: More Left-Handers Go To Hell**

5. **Sir Isaac Newton Fathered 27 Kids**

1. Ghosts Are The Result Of Brain Damage, Says Scientist

TRUTH According to Swiss neuroscientist Peter Brugger of the University Hospital in Zurich, ghosts are not supernatural entities. They're the result of brain damage. You know how amputees can often feel their phantom limbs? Well, in some brain-damaged people, this sensation spreads throughout the entire body, says Brugger. Such people "see" a shadow version of themselves—which they mistakenly believe is a ghost.

2. Viagra Key To Saving Panda From Extinction

TABLOID Scientists have tried just about everything except Viagra to encourage the endangered giant panda to breed more frequently. There are only about fifteen hundred or so pandas left in the wild, due to loss of habitat and the fact that the female panda is in heat for only three days a year.

Male panda: "Honey, wanna fool around?"

Female panda: "I'm not in the mood and won't be for another three hundred sixty-two days."

3. You Can Turn Invisible Spontaneously

TABLOID Santa Barbara hypnotherapist Donna Higbee, though, would likely disagree. Ms. Higbee has been researching "spontaneous invisibility" since the early 1990s and mentions several such cases on a website. For example, a woman named Vera noticed she had turned invisible when a postal clerk spoke right through her to the next person in line. When Vera announced loudly that she was there first, the clerk didn't appear to notice, and Vera ran from the post office in terror.

Postal clerk #1: "Damn! Here comes crazy Vera again. How do I get rid of her?"

Postal clerk #2: "Act like she's invisible."

4. Afterlife Expert: More Left-Handers Go To Hell

TABLOID However, the moral, upstanding right-handed community suspects as much.

5. Sir Isaac Newton Fathered 27 Kids

TABLOID Sir Isaac remained a virgin to his dying day, according to the authoritative *Illustrated Book of Sexual Records*. The book is a "must-read" if you're looking to set a record of your own.

GAME 5

Are the following headlines **TRUTH** *or* **TABLOID?**
(See next page for correct answers.)

1. SCIENTIST FINDS SKID MARKS ON MARS

2. EXPERT: ALIENS FIND EARTH ENTERTAINING

3. LONDON TO BECOME TROPICAL PARADISE

4. HIPPIE AWAKENED FROM COMA BY JANIS JOPLIN LP

5. FALL LEAVES GO INSANE

1. SCIENTIST FINDS SKID MARKS ON MARS

TRUTH After comparing Martian geographical features with those near Antarctica, an American scientist has found them strikingly similar to the "skid marks" left by retreating glaciers. This analysis, completed by Baerbel K. Lucchitta of the United States Geological Society, runs counter to the general belief that the miles-wide markings on Mars's surface were caused by catastrophic flooding.

2. EXPERT: ALIENS FIND EARTH ENTERTAINING

TABLOID Unfortunately, not so. Charles Lineweaver, scientist at the University of New South Wales in Australia, says that earthlings are toddlers in cosmic terms. Alien life forms, he claims, are much more evolved than previously thought, which is why aliens haven't bothered to introduce themselves to us formally. We bore them.

3. LONDON TO BECOME TROPICAL PARADISE

TABLOID C'mon, global warming can't be all bad. I've always imagined the silver lining in that big hole in the ozone would be the chance to spend Christmas sunbathing outside Buckingham Palace.

4. HIPPIE AWAKENED FROM COMA BY JANIS JOPLIN LP

TABLOID Note to younger players: Janis Joplin was a chart-topping sixties singer. However, unlike Britney Spears, Janis drank a quart of Jack Daniel's every day. She was bisexual. She had bad skin. And she didn't do TV commercials. Ms. Joplin died from an overdose of a whole bunch of bad things in 1970.

5. FALL LEAVES GO INSANE

TRUTH Florida International University biologists say that their research indicates fall leaves turn color in a "crazed metamorphosis" to absorb ultraviolet rays better and remain alive a little longer.

GAME 6

Are the following headlines **TRUTH** *or* **TABLOID?**
(See next page for correct answers.)

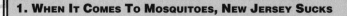

1. WHEN IT COMES TO MOSQUITOES, NEW JERSEY SUCKS

2. MOSQUITO KILLER FOR THE RICH! PLATINUM-PLATED VACUUM

3. $2,000 TIFFANY TENNIS BRACELET "GUARANTEED TO ZAP MOSQUITOES"

4. FLORIDA SUBURB CALLS TWO LOCAL MOSQUITOES "ENDANGERED"

5. MOSQUITO SPIT MAKES PENETRATION EASIER

1. WHEN IT COMES TO MOSQUITOES, NEW JERSEY SUCKS

TRUTH The much-maligned state can't get a break. Of the 150 known species of mosquitoes in the United States, New Jersey is home to 63 of them, including the swamp breeding, floodwater, snowpool, and ever-popular container breeding mosquito.

2. MOSQUITO KILLER FOR THE RICH! PLATINUM-PLATED VACUUM

TRUTH Got eight hundred dollars to spend on a mosquito killer? Look no further than the Mosquito Magnet from the American Biophysics Corporation. The device employs platinum to help create a chemical reaction that lures mosquitoes to it, then sucks them inside and kills them. A "professional model" is available for thirteen hundred dollars.

3. $2,000 TIFFANY TENNIS BRACELET "GUARANTEED TO ZAP MOSQUITOES"

TABLOID You don't have to spend big bucks to own a beautiful anti-mosquito bracelet. A company called BugOff! has a six-dollar lime-green bracelet that uses citronella, geraniol, and lemongrass to scare away mosquitoes.

4. FLORIDA SUBURB CALLS TWO LOCAL MOSQUITOES "ENDANGERED"

TABLOID Unfortunately, the vast supply of mosquito-destroying devices are not threatening the extinction of any of the approximately three thousand species around the world. However, I hear some "mosquito huggers" want to make swatting a capital offense.

5. MOSQUITO SPIT MAKES PENETRATION EASIER

TRUTH When the female mosquito (males don't bite) pierces your skin, she injects a small amount of saliva into the wound before drawing blood. The saliva makes penetration easier and prevents the blood from clotting in the narrow channel of her food canal.

GAME 7

Are the following headlines **TRUTH** *or* **TABLOID?**
(See next page for correct answers.)

1. MORE SEX PARTNERS = LARGER SEX ORGANS

2. LARGER SEX ORGANS = MORE SEX PARTNERS

3. SOON! WOMEN WILL "GROW THEIR OWN" BIGGER BREASTS

4. THAR SHE BLOWS! SCIENTISTS SIGHT GAY DOLPHINS

5. HAND-HELD DEVICE DETERMINES IF YOU'RE SEXY

1. MORE SEX PARTNERS = LARGER SEX ORGANS

TRUTH Don't get too excited. This "truth" applies only to yellow dung flies, according to experts at the University of Zurich. The researchers bred dung flies to be either polygamous or monogamous and found that males and females that came from polygamous lines developed larger sex organs within ten generations.

2. LARGER SEX ORGANS = MORE SEX PARTNERS

TABLOID No truth to that tall tale. I think.

3. SOON! WOMEN WILL "GROW THEIR OWN" BIGGER BREASTS

TRUTH Guys may be more excited about this than gals, but Kevin Cronin of the Institute for Microsurgery in Melbourne, Australia, is developing a technique for growing breast tissue. The method involves implanting a "chamber" containing a scaffold into the breast. Cells from the individual's own breast tissue then migrate to the chamber and grow around the scaffold, which eventually dissolves. The result is an augmentation that is a completely integrated part of the recipient's breast.

4. THAR SHE BLOWS! SCIENTISTS SIGHT GAY DOLPHINS

TRUTH Brazilian scientists on the isle of Fernando de Noronha, twenty-two miles east of Brazil, said they observed twenty-one cases of homosexual relationships among dolphins, including lesbianism. According to researcher Jose Martins, "Observing male dolphins have sex with each other was simpler than observing females, as they had much more evident sexual organs."

5. HAND-HELD DEVICE DETERMINES IF YOU'RE SEXY

TABLOID Called the beer glass, the device has not proven reliable, especially when repeatedly emptied.

GAME 8

Are the following headlines **TRUTH** *or* **TABLOID?**
(See next page for correct answers.)

1. **STEPHEN HAWKING: WE WILL ALL DIE BY BOILING**

2. **RESEARCHER: TO ENSURE A LONG MARRIAGE, HAVE TRIPLETS**

3. **EGYPTIAN MUMMIES HELP FIND CURE FOR THE FLU**

4. **TO IMPROVE MEMORY, WEAR MITTENS WHEN YOU DRIVE**

5. **DEAF WOMAN HEARS WITH HER TONGUE**

1. STEPHEN HAWKING: WE WILL ALL DIE BY BOILING

TRUTH Mr. Hawking, the renowned scientist and author of *A Brief History of Time*, reflected more than a little concern about global warming in a London speech. He said of our planet, "I am afraid the atmosphere might get hotter and hotter until it will be like Venus with boiling sulfuric acid." His suggestion: Colonize other planets. My suggestion: Avoid Venus during summer boiling season.

2. RESEARCHER: TO ENSURE A LONG MARRIAGE, HAVE TRIPLETS

TABLOID After having triplets, it may only seem like you've been together forever. However, this is the advice given by one thoughtful schoolkid in the book *Advice for a Happy Marriage: From Miss Dietz's Third-grade Class*.

3. EGYPTIAN MUMMIES HELP FIND CURE FOR THE FLU

TABLOID About 450 years ago, though, Europeans believed that powder created by grinding up excavated mummies helped to alleviate the symptoms of gout. The practice ended when it was found that some Egyptian mummy powder suppliers were salting the product with the cremated remains of deceased street people.

4. TO IMPROVE MEMORY, WEAR MITTENS WHEN YOU DRIVE

TRUTH Performing ordinary tasks in an unusual manner is a way to "cross-train your brain" and keep mentally sharp, according to the authors of *Keeping Your Brain Alive*, a book on brain fitness. Duke University scientist Dr. Lawrence C. Katz and cowriter Manning Rubin also advocate sniffing vanilla in the morning and eating meals with the wrong hand.

5. DEAF WOMAN HEARS WITH HER TONGUE

TABLOID In truth, a blind woman was found to "see" with her tongue. According to *Science News*, a growing body of research indicates that the tongue may be the second-best place on the body for receiving visual information and transmitting it to the brain. Blind since birth, Marie-Laure Martin displayed her ability for researchers at the University of Wisconsin at Madison. A German inventor has been granted a patent for a tongue-vision system.

GAME 9

Are the following headlines **TRUTH** or **TABLOID?**
(See next page for correct answers.)

1. DEAD BIRDS A GOOD ECOLOGICAL SIGN, SAY EXPERTS

2. SHRIMP KILL BY YAWNING

3. ARMADILLO CARRIES "BRAIN" BETWEEN LEGS

4. DISCOVERED! 600-MILE-LONG ANT COLONY

5. IT'S ALIVE! 250-YEAR-OLD WORM

1. DEAD BIRDS A GOOD ECOLOGICAL SIGN, SAY EXPERTS

TRUTH In Oregon, waves of dead murres washing up on shore are considered a sign that the threatened species had a healthy spring hatch, and that's straight from the mouths of United States Fish and Wildlife biologists. Go figure.

2. SHRIMP KILL BY YAWNING

TABLOID Belching is the shrimp's weapon of mass destruction. According to scientists at the University of Twente in the Netherlands, the gas bubbles that shrimp emit are powerful enough to kill small prey. And physicist Detlef Lohse says that when huge clusters of shrimp belch in unison, the sound is loud enough to disturb the readings of sophisticated sonar.

3. ARMADILLO CARRIES "BRAIN" BETWEEN LEGS

TABLOID Actually, scientists have found that the octopus has centers of intelligence, or brains, between its many legs that allow them to operate independently.

4. DISCOVERED! 600-MILE-LONG ANT COLONY

TRUTH Scientists in California have identified an incredible six-hundred-mile-long supercolony of ants stretching from San Diego to just north of San Francisco. The Argentinian, or sugar, ants first came to the United States in the 1890s aboard ships bringing sugar and coffee from South America. Sugar ants usually battle one another for territory, but because of the genetic uniformity of the California clan, they've worked together over the years to create the monumental colony.

5. IT'S ALIVE! 250-YEAR-OLD WORM

TRUTH It's a fact, and it's disgusting. Over a period of several years, researchers measured tube worms living on the ocean floor off the Louisiana coast. Based on their slow rate of growth, the worms take about 250 years to reach a length of six feet, which is not uncommon.

GAME 10

Are the following headlines **TRUTH** *or* **TABLOID**?
(See next page for correct answers.)

1. **STARTLING PLAN TO "WEAPONIZE" SALMON**

2. **ENVIRONMENTALISTS ATTACK DRACULA**

3. **FEAR AND PANIC LOWER HEART ATTACK RISK**

4. **"HELP ME FEED STARVING UFO ALIENS," ACTIVIST PLEADS**

5. **SNEEZING BEFORE SEX IMPROVES PERFORMANCE**

1. STARTLING PLAN TO "WEAPONIZE" SALMON

TABLOID However, Jens G. Balchen, of the Norwegian University of Science and Technology, is working on an electronic backpack that will help guide pollack to perform underseas errands for us. Tiny electric shocks coming from the backpack will help to steer the pollack in the correct direction. Other fish were considered, but, says Balchen, "Cod are too strong-willed and hard to steer. Salmon are stupid." That's why the pollack, a species that possesses neither of those negative characteristics, was chosen for the assignment.

2. ENVIRONMENTALISTS ATTACK DRACULA

TRUTH A Dracula theme park in Sighisoara, Romania, has come under fire. Environmentalists say the $38-million, 150-acre Dracula Land will destroy a protected oak grove. Some local clergymen contend the amusement park "risks becoming a focus for Satanists, destruction, and curses." Sighisoara is widely regarded as the birthplace of Vlad the Impaler, the real-life tyrant who inspired Bram Stoker's novel *Dracula*.

3. FEAR AND PANIC LOWER HEART ATTACK RISK

TRUTH Research shows that fear can stimulate a preservation instinct in people. "That's what happened during the Second World War; people actually had fewer heart attacks," Dr. Andy Wielgosz, spokesman for Canada's Heart and Stroke Foundation, told the *National Post*. "The will to survive tends to increase with fear."

4. "HELP ME FEED STARVING UFO ALIENS," ACTIVIST PLEADS

TABLOID Lara Johnstone of South Africa *did* go on a month-long hunger strike to force President George W. Bush to explore space "peacefully and cooperatively with all cultures on Earth and in space." Unfortunately for Lara and extraterrestrials, Mr. Bush acted like he never heard of her.

5. SNEEZING BEFORE SEX IMPROVES PERFORMANCE

TABLOID Sneezing is not foreplay. On the other hand, a United States company is developing a nasal spray meant to enhance the sexual performance of both men and women. The spray, which contains a substance called PT-141, acts on the brain to stimulate desire. Be sure not to confuse it with air freshener before your next party.

SOURCES

Nigel Puddingporne combed the world for this collection of Truth or Tabloid? games. Here's a list of sources, as provided on a wet-bar napkin by Nigel:

Current Anthropology, Boston Globe, Willamette Week, Mixer, Current Biology, Journal of the American Medical Association, 60 Minutes, Science, Proceso, American Biophysics, EPA, *U.S. News & World Report, Sydney Morning Herald, International Herald Tribune, Paris Match, Yorkshire Evening Post,* Tug-Of-War International Association, *Seattle Post-Intelligencer,* American College of Nutrition, American Chemical Society, *Indianapolis Star-News, Las Vegas Review-Journal, Journal of Health & Social Behavior,* British Design Council, *MSNBC News.*

Oregon Department of Agriculture, LBC 1152 AM "The Voice of London," *Los Angeles Daily News,* National Public Radio, *Journal of Personality and Social Psychology,* Earth Environment Service, *Geophysical Research Letters,* Radio 1, *New York Times, Wall Street Journal, Oregonian, Register-Guard, Chicago Sun-Times, Chicago Tribune,* CNN, ABC News, NBC News, CBS News, Speed Channel, *Autoweek, Los Angeles Times, Seattle Times, Nature, USA Today, Hollywood Reporter, CBS Marketwatch.*

Surfing The Apocalypse, iafrica.com, Game Show Convention Center, CNews, BBC News, *Times of India,* Reuters, Associated Press, National Institute of Health, *New Scientist, Academic Emergency Medicine, Washington Post, Times of London,* news24.com, *National Post,* Celebrity Bodies, Rent-A-Ghost, Alien Resistance, Ananova.com, *Billboard,* Holland America, *Salon, Glamour, Natural Health,* Fox News.

Tennessean, History Channel, A&E, *Maxim, New York Daily News, Filmfax, Psychotronic Magazine, This Is South Wales, Journal of Neuroscience,* KPAM-AM, *Parade,* Tacoma News-Tribune, Budweiser, *Milwaukee Journal,* American Heart Association, Paintballgear.com, Canadian Half-pints, Nunchaku Society, *Business Traveler, Town & Country, Hunstville Times,* Biospace.com, *Chest,* Mr. Showbiz.com, *Miami Herald, W* magazine, ameracord.com.

ACKNOWLEDGMENTS

Are the following headlines **TRUTH or TABLOID?**

CAROLINE CARNEY CALLED NATION'S HARDEST-WORKING LITERARY AGENT

DORIANNE STEELE DUBBED MANHATTAN'S SHARPEST EDITOR.

ANSWER: EACH HEADLINE IS THE TRUTH.

Nigel Puddingporne thanks both Caroline and Dorianne for helping bring **TRUTH or TABLOID?** to life.